Discovering ancient Crete through the
ARCHAEOLOGICAL MUSEUM OF
HERAKLION

© 2024 KAPON EDITIONS
FIRST EDITION: JUNE 2024
ISBN 978-618-218-046-4

All rights reserved under law 2387/20 (modified under law 2121/93 which is in effect today) and under the Bern Convention (ratified under law 100/1975). This book or parts thereof may not be reproduced in any form, stored in any retrieval system, or transmitted in any form by any means – electronic, mechanical, photocopy, recording, or otherwise – without prior written permission of the publisher.

KAPON EDITIONS
23–27 Makriyanni str., 117 42 Athens, Greece, T 0030 210 9235098

RACHEL'S BOOKSHOP
22 Ploutarchou str., 106 76 Athens, Greece, T 0030 210 9210983

www.kaponeditions.gr • linktr.ee/kapon_editions • info@kaponeditions.gr

GIORGOS RETHEMIOTAKIS

Discovering ancient Crete through the
ARCHAEOLOGICAL MUSEUM OF
HERAKLION

TRANSLATION: DONIERT EVELY

KAPON EDITIONS

CONTENTS

Prologue 9
From the history of the Museum 10
Archaeological - Historical Chart 14
Timeline 19

GROUND FLOOR

STONE AGE. NEOLITHIC PERIOD (7000-3000 BC),
EARLY BRONZE AGE. PREPALATIAL PERIOD (3000-1900 BC)

ROOM I: The First Communities 20
Settlements And Cemeteries 21

MIDDLE BRONZE AGE. LATE PREPALATIAL (2200-1900 BC)
AND PROTOPALATIAL PERIOD (1900-1700 BC)

ROOM II: From Small Communities To Cities 27
ROOM III: The First Palaces 32

LATE BRONZE AGE. THE NEOPALATIAL PERIOD (1700-1450 BC)

ROOM IV: The New Palaces — The Zenith Of Minoan Culture 42
ROOM V: Settlements — Ports — Trade. The Scripts 50
ROOM VI: Private And Public Life — Bread And Spectacles 58
ROOM VII: Minoan Religion — Domestic And Open-Air Cult 70
ROOM VIII: Minoan Religion — Palatial Worship 80

LATE BRONZE AGE. THE NEOPALATIAL PERIOD (1700-1450 BC)
AND FINAL PALATIAL PERIOD (1450-1300 BC)

ROOM IX: The Monopalatial System Of Knossos — A New Dynasty —
The First Greek Script 93
Cemeteries of the Neopalatial-period 96
ROOM X: Cemeteries of the Final Palatial Period —
Monumental Tombs, the Illustrious Dead 100

LATE BRONZE AGE. THE POSTPALATIAL PERIOD (1300-1100 BC)

ROOM XI: Settlements — Sanctuaries — Tombs 108
ROOM XII: Larnakes — The World of the Dead 114

FIRST FLOOR

ROOM XIII: Minoan Murals. The World of the Court and the World of Nature 120
ROOM XIV: Minoan Legacy: Cretan myths to Late Antiquity. Myth And Reality 132
ROOM XXV: Minoan Echoes: Cretan Myths from the Renaissance to the Modern Era 135

GREEK AND ROMAN ERA
GEOMETRIC, ARCHAIC AND CLASSICAL PERIOD (11th–4th centuries BC.)

ROOM XV: Cities And Sanctuaries — The Institutional Basis Of The 'Cretan Polity' 138
ROOM XVI: Trade — Cultural Influences 144
ROOM XVII: The Sanctuaries — From Minoan Cult To The Amalgamation Of Religious Beliefs . . . 146
ROOM XVIII: The Cemetery Of The City Of Prinias 154
ROOM XIX: The Cemeteries 156

CLASSICAL, HELLENISTIC AND ROMAN PERIOD (5th century BC–4th century AD)

ROOM XX: Cities and Sanctuaries 163
ROOM XXI: Cretan Coinage 168
ROOM XXII: The Cemeteries. Inscriptions. International Trade 172
ROOM XXIII: Private Collections: The Collection Of Doctor Stylianos Giamalakis,
The Nikolaos And Theano Metaxa Collection 180
ROOM XXIV: Lecture and audio-visual media room 183

GROUND FLOOR
SCULPTURE (7th–4th centuries BC.)

ROOM XXVI: Archaic Period (7th–6th centuries BC) and Classical Period (5th–4th centuries BC) . . 184
ROOM XXVII: Hellenistic Period (3rd–2nd centuries BC),
Roman Period (1st century BC–4th century AD) 188

Minoan women conversing, seated on a window-ledge: detail from a painted reconstruction of the "Queen's Hall" at Knossos, according to A. Evans, by Emil Gilliéron.

ABOVE A young Cretan woman, among the pithoi of Magazine 12 at Knossos, 1902.

BELOW Living with antiquities: the Eliakis household in Agioi Deka, near Gortyna, in a photograph by Fred Boissonnas in 1919. A Roman sarcophagus can be seen at the entrance, inverted column bases on the staircase and capitals built into the walls.

RIGHT Man in traditional Cretan costume, at the bottom of the Grand Staircase of Knossos, circa 1910.

Prologue

The Archaeological Museum of Heraklion, one of the most important in the country and the largest in Crete, was founded in the early years of the previous century. It houses and displays the material remains and reveals the special character of the ancient civilizations that developed in Crete from the remote past until Late Antiquity and spans seven millennia, from the Neolithic to the Roman era.

Since 2014, after an extension to the building and a radical renovation of the exhibition, its Collections spread across 27 rooms (I-XXVII) encompassing 12,000 exhibits, reaching from the 7th millennium BC until the 4th century AD.

Early times are represented by the exhibits of the Neolithic era, which lasted about four millennia. The uniqueness of the Museum lies, however, in the size and wealth of the Minoan collection that makes up the most extensive section of its exhibition and includes the most famous masterpieces of Minoan art. Thousands of exhibits found in Minoan palaces, settlements and mansions, sanctuaries and cemeteries portray the panorama of the Minoan world and show the singular characteristics of this unique cultural phenomenon of the 3rd and especially the 2nd millennia BC. The collections of the Hellenic years, from the beginning of the 1st millennium BC onwards, include creations of societies different from their Minoan counterparts in the basic elements of their organization but just as distinguished for their innovative artistic perception. The most important exhibits document the integration of Crete in the cultural values of the Greek world and the island's contribution to these values. The Roman collection, no less interesting, reflects the prosperity that Crete experienced as a province of the Roman Empire from 67 BC, enabled by the prevalence of peaceful conditions.

The exhibition develops following the sequence of chronological-historical periods, in parallel with thematic sections and sub-sections. The detailed description of the exhibits, the introductory material and the digital interactive presentations support the exhibition "narrative".

The present archaeological guide of the Heraklion Museum attempts, through the exhibits, to describe the cultural history of Crete for thousands of years and to guide the reader, like a new Ariadne's thread, through the labyrinth of Cretan archaeology, introducing them to aspects of ancient Crete, the land of myth.

Furthermore, it will motivate visitors to tour the important archaeological sites where the exhibits come from. In so doing, they will gaze upon the unique images of the diverse Cretan landscape, lowland, mountainous and coastal – which was the foundation underpinning the special cultural expression of Crete.

From the history of the Museum

1878-1883. When Crete was still under Ottoman rule, the Heraklion Educational Association was founded, with the aim of developing Greek culture on the island. In 1883, the physician and antiquities lover Iosif Hatzidakis becomes president of the Association and then the first director of the Cretan Museum. Under a decree from the sultan, the Association was recognized as a quasi-archaeological authority and undertook the collection of Cretan antiquities and the carrying out of excavations, all with the aim of establishing a Cretan Museum. The first public collection, enriched by donations of antiquities from local private collectors, is thus created. In 1878, art lover and resident of Heraklion Minos Kalokairinos discovers the palace of Knossos and conducts a limited investigation.

1899/1900-1914. The autonomy of Crete under the supervision of the four Great Powers is declared. The Cretan Museum is granted by the Association to the Cretan State (1900-1913). An archaeological law is passed; two archaeological districts are defined with I. Hatzidakis (the Museum-Knossos) and Stefanos Xanthoudides (the countryside) as curators. Intensive archaeological excavations begin by the two men, as well as by foreign archaeological missions that show a keen interest in Cretan antiquities. The great Minoan palaces and ancient cities are revealed, mainly in central and eastern Crete. Large-scale excavations by the British archaeologist Arthur Evans begin in Knossos and they are to last for decades. The collections of the Cretan Museum are constantly enriched with new rich finds.

1904-1908. A single museum hall with a structure at the rear is erected, in a prominent position in the centre of Heraklion, just inside the eastern Venetian wall, at the site of the ruins of the famous Venetian monastery of Agios Franciscos and the Franciscan order.

1912. A western wing and a classicist façade are added to the building, in the general spirit of the classicist style by Panagis Kavvadias and the well-known architect-archaeologist Wilhelm Dörpfeld.

1913-1914 and following. Crete is united to Greece. Excavations expand, especially after the period of the First World War, and archaeological collections are growing. The Museum's library is established.

1923-1933. The Museum building is pronounced insufficient in terms of space, but also in terms of stability, after serious damage due to strong earthquakes. After the retirement of J. Hatzidakis (1923) and the death of St. Xanthoudides (1928), the request for the construction of a new, modern Museum is promoted by the next curator, Spyridon Marinatos. Plans are prepared by architect Patroklos Karantinos for a new earthquake-proof building of the Museum, with an area of 8,800 sq.m.

1934, 1937-1939, 1958. The new Museum is gradually taking shape in the site of the previous building. It is a pioneering piece of architecture in terms of form and functionality, an important work of the "new architecture" of the Interwar period, and recognized internationally as one of the most representative "exhibition and leisure" buildings in Europe.

1941-1945. Upon the War's outbreak, the antiquities are transferred to safe secret shelters under the supervision of curator Nikolaos Platon. The Museum building was commandeered by the German occupation administration and housed various departments.

OPPOSITE PAGE LEFT Conservation of antiquities by the craftsmen in the first workshop of the Museum, in the presence of Director Joseph Hatzidakis.
OPPOSITE PAGE RIGHT The first museum exhibition of Cretan antiquities in Heraklion, in the early years of the previous century.
ABOVE Joseph Hatzidakis (1848-1936), founder of the archaeological collections and first Director of the Heraklion Museum.

1951-1952. New storerooms are built. The re-exhibition of the collections that were stored during the Second World War is implemented by the ephor curator Nikolaos Platon.

1964-1973. The ephor curator Stylianos Alexiou completes the exhibition, arranges the new wing with four more rooms and organizes the Scientific Collection on the first floor of the building, a parallel exhibition accessible to researchers of Cretan antiquity. From 1973 onwards, after the establishment of museums and archaeological collections in western and eastern Crete, the Museum is now enriched with finds only from central Crete.

1977-2001. The archaeological wealth of the Museum is constantly strengthened with findings from new excavations by the Ephorate of Antiquities of Heraklion under the direction of the ephors Yiannis Sakellarakis, Charalambos Kritzas and Alexandra Karetsou. The need for the renovation of the exhibition and the building is becoming increasingly imperative.

2000-2003. The planning for the renovation-modernization of the Museum is pushed forward, following the architectural and static study by the Al. Tombazis architectural practice. Ground-breaking and construction work begins. The discovery of the ruins of the Venetian monastery of Agios Franciscos in the garden of the Museum causes the work to be stopped and put on hold. Excavation by the Ephorate of Byzantine and Post-Byzantine Antiquities follows.

2003-2008. In 2003, the Museum is administratively separated from the Ephorate of Antiquities of Heraklion. It is organized as a new, independent Directorate with Nota Dimopoulou as its first Director. The re-exhibition project is part of the Eu-

LEFT Pages from A. Evans' 1896 diary, with notes on antiquities seen on his trip to Crete. Painted reconstructions of the Grand Staircase of Knossos by Christian Dole, 1905.

RIGHT A. Evans among finds from his excavations at Knossos. Portrait painted in 1907 by Sir William Richmond.

OPPOSITE PAGE A. Evans' multi-volume work "The Palace of Minos at Knossos" (1921-1935), a fundamental work of Minoan archaeology.

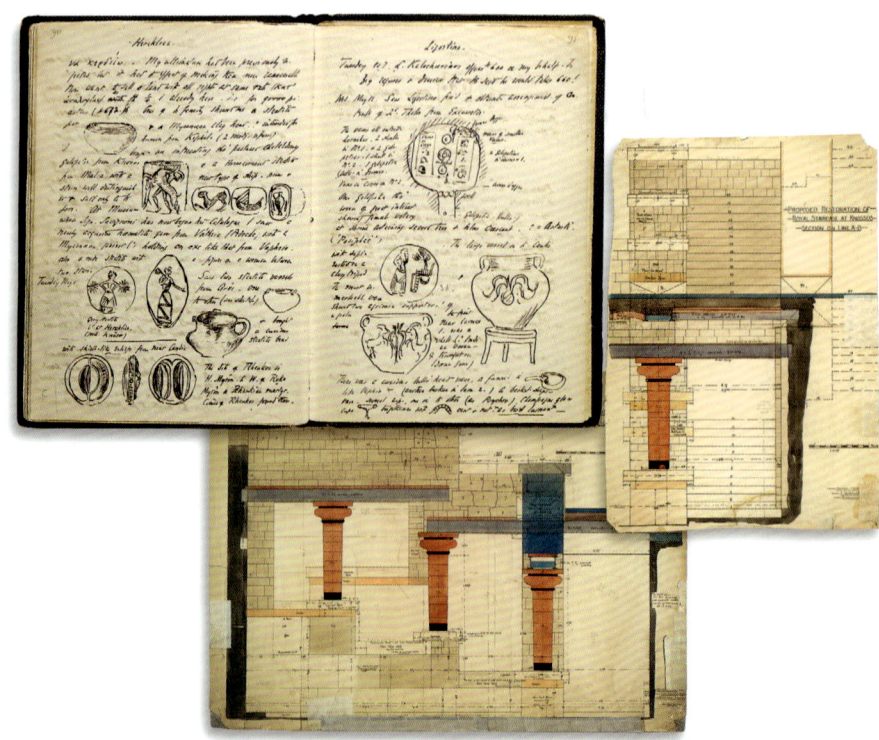

ropean funding program (3rd CPS). Museological studies are prepared and the digital documentation and storage-classification of the entire archaeological collection of the Museum, which numbers hundreds of thousands of objects, is carried out.

The Museum closes to the public in November 2006, the offices and laboratories are relocated to the new extension buildings.

In 2007, a temporary exhibition is organized for public viewing, with selected exhibits in a specially designed area of the extension buildings.

2009-2014. A museological study is prepared, based on the final re-exhibition study. The implementation of the project of the re-exhibition of the Collections with European Community funding (3rd CPS, ESPA) is promoted, which includes the supply of display cases, the conservation of the exhibits, the layout of the garden, as well as the presentation of the ruins of the Agios Franciscos monastery.

Under the direction of Giorgos Rethemiotakis, the re-exhibition was completed in successive phases: Exhibition of Sculptures (2012), Exhibition of Murals (2012-2013), Exhibition of the Greek-Roman Collection (2013), Exhibition of the Prehistoric-Minoan Collection (2014). The renovated Museum with 12,000 exhibits in 27 rooms was opened to the public on May 5, 2014. The official opening took place on June 21, 2014.

2017-. Special praise was bestowed in 2017 on the renovated Museum, which was under the direction of St. Mandalaki at the time, by the internationally established "Museum of the Year Award" of the Council of Europe. In 2023, a new administrative framework was set up under a Director General and a Council led by a President. The Museum hosts temporary exhibitions, educational programs, guided tours and other cultural activities.

Archaeological - Historical Chart

PREHISTORIC CRETE — THE MINOAN WORLD (7th MILLENNIUM BC-1100 BC)

The distinctive cultural identity of Crete is considered to owe a lot to its particular geographical and advantageous position. Set in the centre of the eastern Mediterranean, at the crossroads of the sea routes between three continents of Europe, Asia and Africa, Crete has always been a hub for the network connecting people, goods, ideas, artistic and technological innovations, and the island made fruitful use of diverse cultural stimuli. At the same time, its geographical isolation, in the middle of a sea that unites but also divides, was combined with self-sufficiency in production and aided by the historical circumstances of the era. These elements promoted the creation of an original and recognizable cultural expression. Although recent research on the southern coast of Crete has pushed back the dawn of Cretan prehistory to the Palaeolithic era of about 100,000 years ago, the oldest known permanent installations belong to the Neolithic era, from the 7th to the 4th millennia BC. The first hunters and gatherers gradually settled and evolved into farmers and stock breeders, developing the first cultivated plant species and raising tamed domestic animals. Members of the Neolithic communities used tools made of stone and bone.

In the end of the 4th and the beginning of the 3rd millennia BC, the then revolutionary technology of processing and using metals, mainly copper, was introduced to Crete, marking the transition from the Stone Age to the Bronze Age, accompanied by rapid cultural developments. The decisive change seems to be relat-

ed to the arrival of new settlers from the Cyclades, who together with the old population base formed the dynamic spark of the brilliant Minoan civilization. This first period of its genesis and formation during the 3rd millennium BC is called Prepalatial, because it precedes the establishment of palaces. The settlements increase, the commercial activities expand and the agricultural economy develops, as does the artisanal output thanks to the new tools and equipment made of metal. Shipping and trade fuelled production by bringing in materials and know-how, further contributing to the vigorous development of the arts. In the mature phases of the period, factors like the continuous economic blooming, the organization of production, the creation of large settlements with features of 'urbanization' and elements of an administrative structure seem to have favoured the emergence of powerful social groups, classes and perhaps local chiefs. Political-social realities and favorable economic conditions eventually led to the establishment of the first palaces at the beginning of the 2nd millennium BC, a development that defines the beginning of the Protopalatial period. The first palaces were erected within cities, which developed into an urban fabric at important Prepalatial settlements. The largest ones are in Knossos, Phaistos and Malia in central Crete, while smaller ones exist in Petras, Sitia and Monastiraki in Rethymnon. They are the seats of the rulers of a particular region in the wider hinterland, centres of secular and religious power, with an administrative and economic organization, and using bureaucratic systems involving writing and sealing practices. The first palaces were destroyed around 1700 BC from natural causes, likely earthquakes and fire. However, new palaces were constructed in their place, bigger and more luxurious, while others were added, such as that of Zakros in eastern Crete and Galatas in central Crete. The complex Minoan palatial system reached its apex in this period – the Neopalatial, and was the driving force for the Minoan expansion throughout the Aegean and Eastern Mediterranean area. Strong secular and religious power emanating from the palaces ensured the system's internal stability and social cohesion, by systematizing and controlling production and trade, alongside developing mechanisms of ideological control and guidance through religion and the organization of public spectacles. At the same time, the palaces coordinated the activities of the powerful Minoan fleet, the 'sea power', in the words of Thucydides. Through a network of colonies, outposts and commercial ports the system promoted the reach of Minoan Crete, bringing the glamour of Minoan art to the royal courts of the East and Egypt. It is the era that left a strong imprint to posterity through the myths and references to the demigod Mi-

BOTTOM **Part of a fresco from Knossos, depicting olive branches (Room VI).**

nos, king of Knossos, son of Zeus and Europa, to the well-ruled Crete, cradle of the arts, and to the Minoan sovereignty of the seas. Around 1530 BC, according to conventional dating, the eruption of biblical proportions of the Thera volcano caused the destruction of the local Cycladic-Minoan city, covering it in layers of ash and brought on the broader devastation of facilities across the Aegean as well as in Crete, without however totally destabilizing the system at that point. The Minoan civilization went on for a century before it collapsed at its peak, around 1450 BC, probably due to internal political-social causes. A new dynasty immediately established itself at Knossos during the Final Palatial period from 1450 to 1300 BC, succeeded by another in Kydonia, (modern Chania) that lasted until 1250 BC. The newcomers controlled a busy bureaucracy written in Mycenaean, the first script in the Greek language. When the last palaces disappeared during the Postpalatial period, cores of social and religious life survived, decentralized now in small communities. At the turn from the 2nd to the 1st millennia BC, these gradually welcomed and assimilated the cultural and political structures of the broader Greek world.

CRETE FROM THE EARLY IRON AGE TO LATE ANTIQUITY. FROM THE DORIANS TO THE ROMANS (11th CENTURY BC–4th CENTURY AD).

After the dissolution of the Creto-Mycenaean world at the end of the 2nd millennium BC, Crete gradually received new population elements, the Greek tribes collectively called 'Dorian'. These progressively merged with the local population and formed the first political and social structures of what becomes the Cretan Polity. The basic expression of this is autonomous cities that control an area proportional to their power. New forms of power emerge, with corresponding public offices, establishing legal codes for the welfare and stability of the state, as well as for the education of the young, which together form the core of the Polis, the Cretan political institutions. The introduction of iron gives new possibilities for tools and war equipment. The worship of the Greek pantheon is consolidated and the Homeric custom of cremation instead of burials is established as a common practice. Crete during the Geometric and Archaic periods experienced great economic and cultural prosperity, especially in the 8th and 7th centuries BC. Trade contacts with the East intensify, the arts flourish, especially sculpture with its original creations, and the first alphabet of the Greek language is introduced, borrowed from the merchant people, the Phoenicians. From the 5th century BC, the first coins are issued, a reality giving new impetus to commercial transactions. But unlike the other Greek cities, the stationary aristocratic polity in Crete never transformed into political systems such as tyranny and democracy. Thus, Crete was gradually isolated, taking gradual steps backwards in terms of culture during the Classical times, in the 5th-4th centuries BC. It was exhausted by civil strife, especially in the Hellenistic period during the 3rd-2nd centuries BC. In 67 BC, it was conquered by the Romans and turned into a Roman province with Gortyna as its capital. Then it experienced a fresh surge in prosperity, with populous cities, adorned with imposing public buildings and luxurious private residences. Its strategic position and ports were particularly exploited for the development of international trade. The peaceful conditions that generally prevailed, the famous Pax Romana, created conditions of affluence and comfortable living with refined manners of behaviour and a love of beauty, in line with the standards that applied to the urban culture of the vast Roman Empire. In 365 AD, a devastating earthquake levelled Cretan cities, causing a general recession. From the 4th century AD, the new religion, Christianity, gradually prevailed. The Arab invasions in the 7th century AD caused the final collapse of the ancient Cretan cities and eliminated all the structures that had belonged to the organized public and private life of Late Antiquity.

BELOW Isis-Persephone and Serapis-Pluto with the three-headed dog Cerberus, a complex of statues discovered in 1913-1914 by the Italian archaeologist G. Oliveiro in the temple of the Egyptian Deities in Gortyna. In the Museum's Sculpture Hall (XXVII), the statues are displayed as a central exhibit (fig. 321).

0 | GROUND FLOOR
**MINOAN COLLECTION
SCULPTURE**

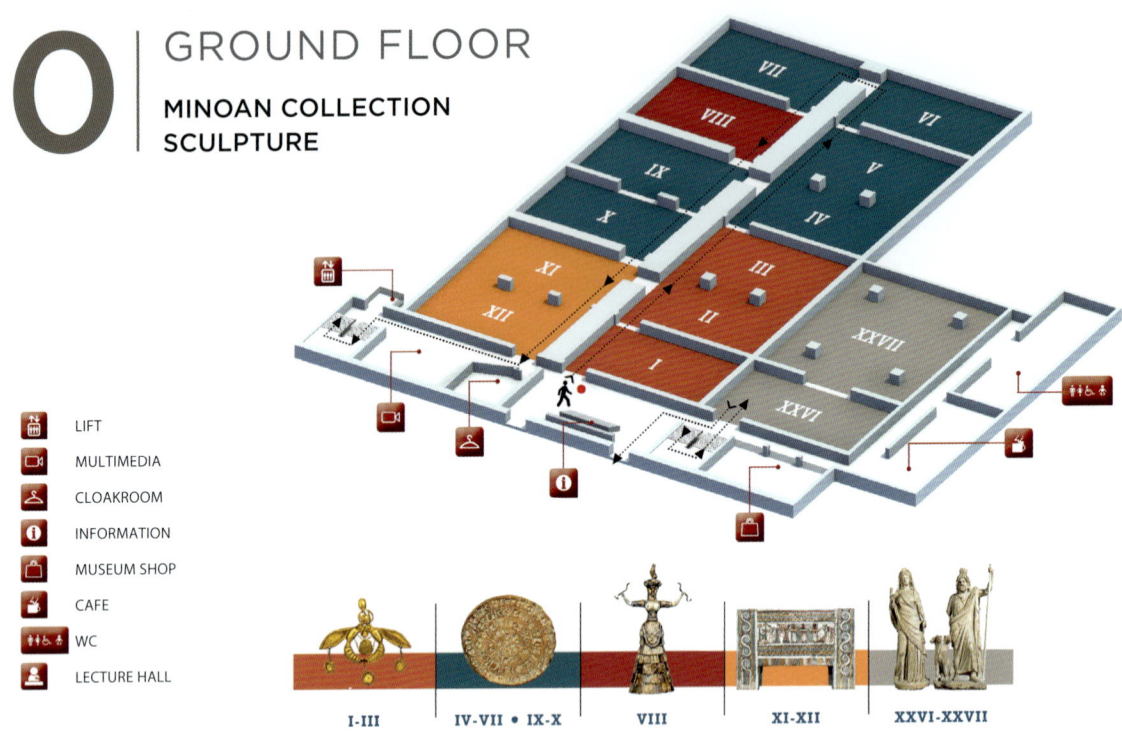

- LIFT
- MULTIMEDIA
- CLOAKROOM
- INFORMATION
- MUSEUM SHOP
- CAFE
- WC
- LECTURE HALL

| I-III | IV-VII • IX-X | VIII | XI-XII | XXVI-XXVII |

1 | FIRST FLOOR
**MINOAN WALL PAINTINGS
GREEK - ROMAN COLLECTION**

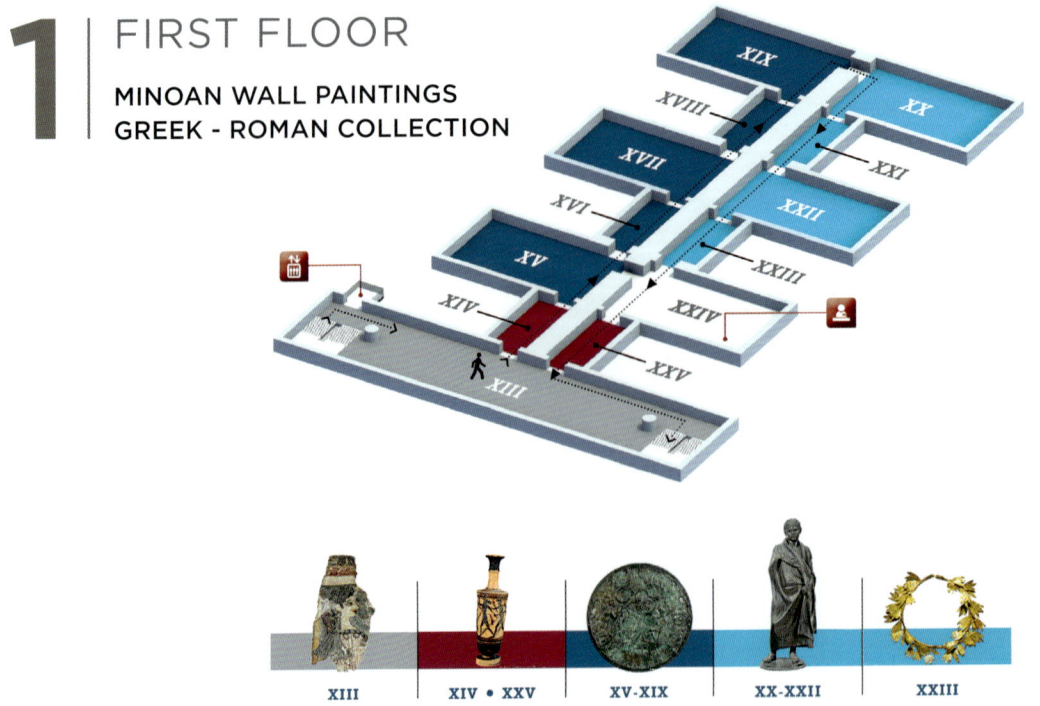

| XIII | XIV • XXV | XV-XIX | XX-XXII | XXIII |

TIMELINE

NEOLITHIC PERIOD (ROOM I)

ACERAMIC PERIOD
7000/6800–6500 BC

EARLY NEOLITHIC PERIOD
6500–5800 BC

MIDDLE NEOLITHIC PERIOD
5800–5300 BC

LATE NEOLITHIC PERIOD
5300–4500 BC

FINAL NEOLITHIC (SUB-NEOLITHIC) PERIOD
4500–3200/3000 BC

EARLY BRONZE AGE (ROOMS I-II)

PREPALATIAL PERIOD
EARLY MINOAN I
3200/3000–2600 BC

EARLY MINOAN II
2600–2300 BC

EARLY MINOAN III
2300–2100 BC

MIDDLE BRONZE AGE (ROOMS II-III)

PROTOPALATIAL PERIOD
MIDDLE MINOAN I
2100–1900 BC

MIDDLE MINOAN II
1900–1700 BC

LATE BRONZE AGE (ROOMS IV-XII)

NEOPALATIAL PERIOD
MIDDLE MINOAN III
1700–1580 BC

LATE MINOAN I A-B
1580–1450 BC

FINAL PALATIAL PERIOD
LATE MINOAN II-IIIA
1450–1350/1300 BC

POSTPALATIAL PERIOD
LATE MINOAN IIIB-IIIC
1350/1300–1070 BC

SUBMINOAN PERIOD
1070–1000 BC

**GREEK AND ROMAN ERA
(ROOMS XV-XXII, XXVI-XXVII)**

PROTOGEOMETRIC I PERIOD
1000–850 BC
PROTOGEOMETRIC II PERIOD
850–810 BC
GEOMETRIC PERIOD
810–700 BC
ORIENTAL OR DAEDALIC
OR EARLY ARCHAIC PERIOD
700–600 BC
ARCHAIC PERIOD
600–500 BC
CLASSICAL PERIOD
500–323 BC
HELLENISTIC PERIOD
323–67 BC
ROMAN PERIOD
67 BC–4TH CENTURY AD

ROOM I
Stone Age. Neolithic Period (7000–3000 BC)

THE FIRST COMMUNITIES. NEOLITHIC KNOSSOS

The Neolithic period is marked by the use of stone as the material for the manufacture of tools of various uses. The transition from the stage of hunting and food gathering to the organization of the first agricultural settlements takes place during this period. Cultivation of the land is developed and systematized, animals are domesticated in order to give their products and thus ensure the self-sufficiency of communities. The techniques of making clay vessels and textiles are discovered and developed. Evidence of early navigation and trade as early as the 7th millennium BC is witnessed by the recovery in Knossos of Melian obsidian, a volcanic glass naturally present on that island and suitable for creating small tools.

The oldest, largest and longest-lived of all the Neolithic settlements is that of Knossos: it developed in the same area as the palace later on. Settlements also developed throughout Crete, including Katsambas near Knossos, Phaistos and Magasa near Sitia. The houses have stone foundations, with the walls and roofs made of clay and perishable materials; they are generally small in size, with but rudimentary living quarters. Caves such as those of Amnisos, Miamou, Platyvola, among others, were also used for living.

CASES 1-3. UTENSILS – TOOLS

Stone and bone tools, grinders, axes, maceheads and awls were used to grind grain for flour, cultivate the land and in a range of other domestic and technical tasks. Clay spindle-whorls and 'shuttles' were employed for weaving and making clothes. The vessels and utensils for cooking – such as the two portable ovens from Knossos from the late Neolithic period, and others for carrying food and liquids are all simple and handmade. They were fired over an open fire (without the benefit of a kiln), they carry a few incised or painted decorations. Vessels suitable for drawing and transporting water were found inside a deep well cut into the bedrock, at Fourni in Mirabello.

CASE 4. FIGURINES

Clay and stone figurines representing people and animals give solid form to ideological concepts and social values. They represent concerns like the fertility of women and the

guaranteeing of sufficient returns from the plants and animal capital of the land – all of which were basic conditions for the survival of Neolithic communities. The most important figurine is a marble one from Knossos, of 6100-5900 BC. The rendering of anatomy at such an early age is quite remarkable. Also unique is the large seated clay figurine (**Fig. 1**) from Pano Chorio in the Ierapetra region: the particularly accentuated buttocks are a direct reference to the woman's fertility. It is dated to 5800-4500 BC. A clay model of a boat, from the same period, attests to the development of the means of communication overseas.

The Early Bronze Age. Prepalatial period (3000–1900 BC)

CASES 5, 6. SETTLEMENTS AND CEMETERIES

On the turn from the 3rd to the 2nd millennia BC, trade networks with the Aegean and the Near East gradually expanded and consolidated. At the same time, the use of metals, mainly copper, is exploited for the production of objects that meet daily as well as ideological needs, as the acquisition and display of prestigious objects grew. Settlements penetrate towards the inland, and villages are more and better organized than before.

Burial practices by families and clans are structured around large vaulted tombs, mainly in the area of Mesara in central Crete, and in house-like tombs in eastern Crete, especially Mochlos. Cycladic-type pit tombs are known too in Gournes and Agia Fotia near Sitia. A type of clay chest or sarcophagus for depositing the dead, like the one from the Pyrgos cave-tomb in Nirou Hani – appears in this period. Pottery-making techniques, now employing kilns, are also improved, with new shapes and ways of decoration being invented. Three decorative styles are distinguished: burnishing, as in the large biconical chalices of the Pyrgos type; secondly, the Vasilki style boasts mottled black-red spots on its surface, created in the kiln by uneven, but controlled firing (**Fig. 2**; Case 5); and the third technique relies on sets of painted and intersecting fine lines, represented by the Koumasa and Agios Onoufrios styles (**Fig. 3**; Case 6). Earlier ceramic types are still preserved for everyday household utensils, as shown by the portable oven from Agia Triada.

1. Clay Neolithic figurine. Pano Chorio, Ierapetra, 5800-4500 BC.

2. Vasiliki-style jug with 'flame' decoration. Vasiliki, 2600-2300 BC.

3. Jugs in the Koumasa and Agios Onoufrios styles, with linear decoration. Tombs from central Crete, 2600-2300 BC.

CASES 7, 8. THE VAULTED TOMBS OF MESARA

A series of vaulted tombs from the Prepalatial and Protopalatial periods have been excavated in many sites, chiefly in Mesara in south-central Crete. The larger tombs with the richest finds are those from Platanos, Koumasa and Lenda (Lebena) (**Fig. 4**), the latter being on the southern coast-line. These circular tholoi are made of large stones according to the corbel system, so that their walls curve inwards, diminishing in diameter as they rise in height. The tombs usually have external burial rooms and outdoor areas for collecting older interments and for purposes of worship. In the graves were found numerous clay vases, seals and gold jewellery, necklaces of stone beads, stone and clay utensils (**Fig. 5**) with multiple depressions for receiving offerings and small stone slabs, or 'palettes', perhaps for preparing pigments, as well as some ritual utensils and figurines in animal and bird forms (**Fig. 6**).

5

CASE 9. STONE VESSELS

The Minoan artisans working on stone were keenly engaged in the production of vessels, usually of small size and using soft or harder stones alike. The variety of their shapes, colours and decoration achieved by just exploiting the veining (**Fig. 7**), as well as the raw materials included are impressive, which testifies to the vision and skill of the craftsmen. The series

4

of small vases from the tombs at Mochlos and three special vases of chlorite stand out: the pyxis with a lid (for holding jewellery) from Zakros and the lid of another one from Mochlos with similar handles in the form of a recumbent dog in relief, certainly the work of the same craftsman; the third vase is a biconical pyxis with an all-over net of relief spirals from Maronia, Sitia (Fig. 8).

4. Peculiar vases from tombs in Lenda (Lebena), 2800-2500 BC.

5. Clay kernoi for multiple offerings. Tombs from central Crete, 3000-2500 BC.

6. Figurine of a goat, depicted in naturalistic movement. Tomb at Porti, Mesara, 2500-2000 BC.

7. Stone vessels from tombs at Mochlos and central Crete, 2500-1800 BC.

8. Stone pyxis (jewellery case) with relief spirals. Stone pyxis and lid with similar handles in the form of a reclining dog. Tombs from eastern Crete, 2500-2000 BC.

CASE 10. DAGGERS, BRONZE TOOLS

The adoption of moulding techniques led to the production of many metal objects, mainly of copper and its alloys, such as daggers, chisels and axes. The rarity and value of this metal, which in Crete was imported through trade, leads us to safely assume that the owners and users of these objects were limited to the upper classes. This aspect of rank and eliteness is more evident in the silver daggers which are prestige objects.

FIGURINES

Ideological-religious concepts are imported along with different materials, and they become evident in the form of figurines of well-known Cycladic types made of marble or stone. These appear alongside pebble-shaped and schematic figurines, such as the sizeable example from Sambas. Of the 'canonical' Cycladic figurines, with their arms folded across the stomach, those of the Koumasa variant are the most common: they are considered to be local Cretan products. Those of the Spedos type, however, are imported from the Cyclades. A variation of the Cycladic non-standard type is the fine marble seated figurine (**Fig. 9-10**), as well as the pair of smaller figurines – both from Tekes in the Knossos area.

CASE 11. TRADE – FOREIGN INFLUENCES

The range of external trade relations and contacts is documented through a series of exhibits: miniature stone vases reproducing Egyptian types, seals, scarabs and amulets with ideological symbolism referencing Egypt (**Fig. 11**), a rare necklace of silver beads, perhaps of Eastern origin, figurines of Cycladic type and clay vessel types with parallels in the Cyclades, the northern Aegean and north-eastern Asia Minor. Imported raw materials also include obsidian, the volcanic glass used in the production of tools, from Melos in the Cyclades. A typical set of obsidian finds comprises cores, flakes and blades, as well as debitage (that is the raw material, the debris from the processing and the desired end product), as found in workshops of the coastal Prepalatial installation in Poros, Heraklion. The two models of ships from Palaikastro and Mochlos depict the actual vessels carrying the imported products, raw materials – as well as the ideas that fertilized the Cretan creative vein in developing the

9-10

11

24

open and cosmopolitan societies of the Minoan palaces during the following period.

CASE 12 (CENTRAL). GOLD

Gold in Crete was an exclusively imported precious material, and therefore has always been an indication of wealth and social superiority. Many gold objects were found in tombs, mostly in coastal Mochlos, a settlement that grew rich from sea trade in the Prepalatial period, and in the tholos tombs of Mesara. Typically, bands and diadems, olive or myrtle leaves in gold, daisies and thin, elaborately woven chains of wire adorned the head, body and clothing of the distinguished dead (**Fig. 12**). Diadems with repoussé representations of animals and eyes stand out, as does the cylindrical bead from Kalathiana decorated with spirals of fine wire in the so-called filigree technique (**Fig. 13**).

Noteworthy is the tiny gold bead in the form of a frog (**Fig. 14**) from Koumasa which is decorated on its back with gold globules, in the granulation technique. It is dated to 2000-1800 BC, and is considered the earliest example of this technique in Crete.

The necklaces with various beads of gold and semi-precious stones are equally impressive (**Fig. 15**).

9-10. Marble Cycladic figurine of the Spedos type and seated Cycladic figurine. Koumasa and the Knossos area, 2500-2300 BC.

11. Bone seal-amulet in the shape of a fly, with Egyptian parallels. Archanes, 2000-1800 BC.

12. Golden daisies, leaves hanging from chains and two beads with impressed decoration. Mochlos, 2500-2200 BC.

13. Gold bead with spiral filigree decoration. Kalathiana, 2000-1800 BC.

14. Small bead in the form of a frog with gold granulation. Koumasa, 2000-1800 BC.

CASE 13 (CENTRAL). THE SEALS

The seals first appearing in the Prepalatial period constitute an aspect of their owner's identity, but perhaps they also operate as talismans. They are made of soft stones, artificial mixtures of materials, but also of hippopotamus tooth, all materials imported from Egypt and the East. The shapes are varied, including three-sided or four-sided prisms, cylinders or rings. Subjects appearing on their sealing surface either derive from nature (**Fig. 16**) or serve decorative purposes. A special category is the so-called theriomorphic seals, real masterpieces of small-scale artwork. Figures of animals or birds, such as heads of snakes and boars, monkeys, hares and calves, are rendered with imagination and artistic freedom.

15. Gold pendant and necklaces of gold and semi-precious stones; the bead of a bull's head in the centre is of amethyst. Tombs of Mesara and Mochlos, 2300-1500 BC.

16. Bone seal-talisman (and impression) depicting scorpions. Platanos, 2000-1800 BC.

17. Bowl with attached figurines, representing a herd of animals with their shepherd. Palaikastro, 2000-1800 BC

18. Added relief decoration for a vase in the form of a sphinx, with Egyptian influences. Malia, 1800-1700 BC.

ROOM II
Middle Bronze Age. Late Prepalatial (2200–1900 BC) and Protopalatial Period (1900–1700 BC)

FROM SMALL COMMUNITIES TO CITIES

The first large cities in Minoan Crete gradually developed at the turn from the third to the second millennium BC. A typical case is the Protopalatial city of Malia, with its cobbled streets, blocks of housing and large luxury buildings. At the same time, outdoor worship is organized on mountains and hilltops where rituals and offerings take place. Burials continue to take place in tholos tombs; the built burial enclosure of Malia, with the interments in pit tombs, is a special case.

CASE 14. REGIONAL COMMUNITIES

Aspects of life in the regional communities are illuminated by finds from Palaikastro, Sitia. Animal and human figurines affixed to the interior of a small bowl represent a herd with its shepherd (**Fig. 17**). Similar bowls with effigies of many small loaves, small animals or birds on the inside were probably intended as offerings to the deity, representing and replacing the actual offerings themselves. The clay effigy of a four-wheeled cart that would have been drawn by oxen and used to transport loads over an organized road network is an example of this type of object.

17

CASES 15, 16. THE EMERGENCE OF PALATIAL SOCIETIES — SETTLEMENTS AND HOUSES

The residential complex M in the city of Malia is an illuminating example of the complex architectural structure of a large urban house put to a variety of uses and functions, such as reception and worship spaces, storage areas and workshops. Some indicative cases of domestic and artisan activities are the bronze utensils for cooking, stone moulds for making bronze tools, potter's wheels for the production of clay vessels, clay loom weights and spindle whorls for weaving and spinning, as well as a heavy clay tool with a handle, perhaps for polishing the plaster on the surface of walls. The vases from

18

Malia have an individual style, with their 'Egyptianizing' relief additions of ornamental intent, such as the Cretan sphinx (**Fig. 18**) with an Osiris-type beard à la égyptienne, the cats and falcons portrayed on a lid, as well as Egyptian motifs (**Fig. 19**). The tall tripod 'fruit bowls' with their delicate decoration in white are quite unique (**Fig. 20**).

White decorative motifs also characterize the vases that come from workshops in eastern Crete, the first polychrome motifs in white and orange paint also appear. Characteristic of the early Protopalatial period is the penchant for imitating metal models, both in the overall shape and its thin walls, as well as in the colouring given to the clay vessels that imitates bronze – as seen in the ceramics of the workshops of Kastelli, Pediada. The cup-kernos with a pleated rim (**Fig. 21**) displays particular originality and technical skill. It emanates from Myrtos-Pyrgos, with identical miniature cups stuck to its interior.

From the Chamaizi Residence in Sitia, the seat of a local lord in control of the region, come three large clay figurines adopting a worshipping posture.

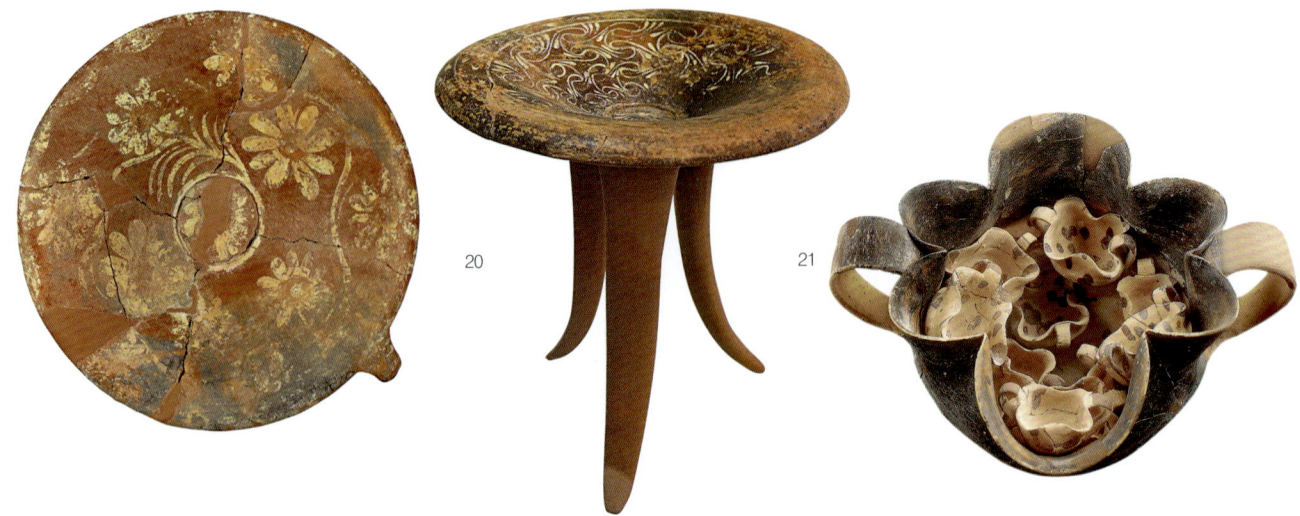

23

CASES 17-18. THE ARCHANES CEMETERY

A cemetery of the nearby Minoan settlement was established on the Fourni hillside, where it was active for over a thousand years, from 2500 to 1350/1300 BC. It includes tombs of various types from all periods. From a tholos tomb's built ossuaryies of the Prepalatial to Protopalatial period aimed for collecting bones and depositing the remains of older burials, come a clay model of a bronze sistrum, the Egyptian musical instrument that produced a rhythmic sound when its disks rattled and shook, as well as gold and ivory jewellery (**Fig. 22**) seals and ritual vessels, and a series of Cycladic figurines testifying again to contacts and influences from the Cyclades.

CASE 19. FUNERARY STRUCTURE OF CHRYSOLAKKOS, MALIA

A little north of the palace, a cemetery was founded around 1800 BC for the leading classes of the city of Malia, as shown by the architectural form employed and the rich finds — at least those spared from pillage. The name of the location – Chrysolakkos (the Gold Pit) – was given to denote the wealth looted by clandestine diggers in the 19th century. The cemetery consists of a cluster of pit graves and an altar for worshipping the dead, set within a built enclosure with an external portico.

Here was found the most famous of Minoan jewels, the gold pendant amulet depicting two bees (**Fig. 23**). The two insects face each other, embracing with their feet a round 'honeycomb' represented by a dense pattern of granulation of soldered microscopic globules. A wire cage enclosing a gold sphere rests on their heads, while circular elements dangle from their wings and conjoined tails. Its creation combined all known techniques of goldsmithing: embossing, engraving, filigree and granulation. The wealth of the burials is further confirmed by the gold hair pin crowned with a flower, small pendants and many fine rectangular and ribbon-shaped gold sheets from the embellishments of the funeral garments.

19. Lid with opposed falcons in relief, an Egyptian theme. Malia, 1800-1700 BC.

20. Tripod 'fruit bowls' with white floral decoration. Malia, 1800-1700 BC.

21. Cup-kernos with pleated rim and small cups inside for receiving offerings. Myrtos, 1900-1800 BC.

22. Necklaces of gold, ivory and a central bead of green stone. Fourni Archanes, 2000-1800 BC.

23. The famous gold amulet of the bees, a masterpiece of Minoan goldsmithing. Malia, 1800-1700 BC.

CASE 20. OTHER CEMETERIES

Interesting offerings come from the tholos tombs of Mesara and the house-type tombs of Gournia. Continuing from the end of the Prepalatial period, the habit of individual burial in sarcophagi expands, as may be witnessed in the tholos tomb at Vorou, where the chests have multiple handles for their carrying and placement in the tomb, by using straps or ropes. Gifts worthy of the above tombs are the silver kantharos from Gournia, a metal vase shape copied in many similar clay ones, some of which are also exhibited. The small models of winepresses from the tombs at Apesokari in the Mesara are also quite interesting: they lend a direct reference to an important process, the pressing of grapes by foot and the production of wine.

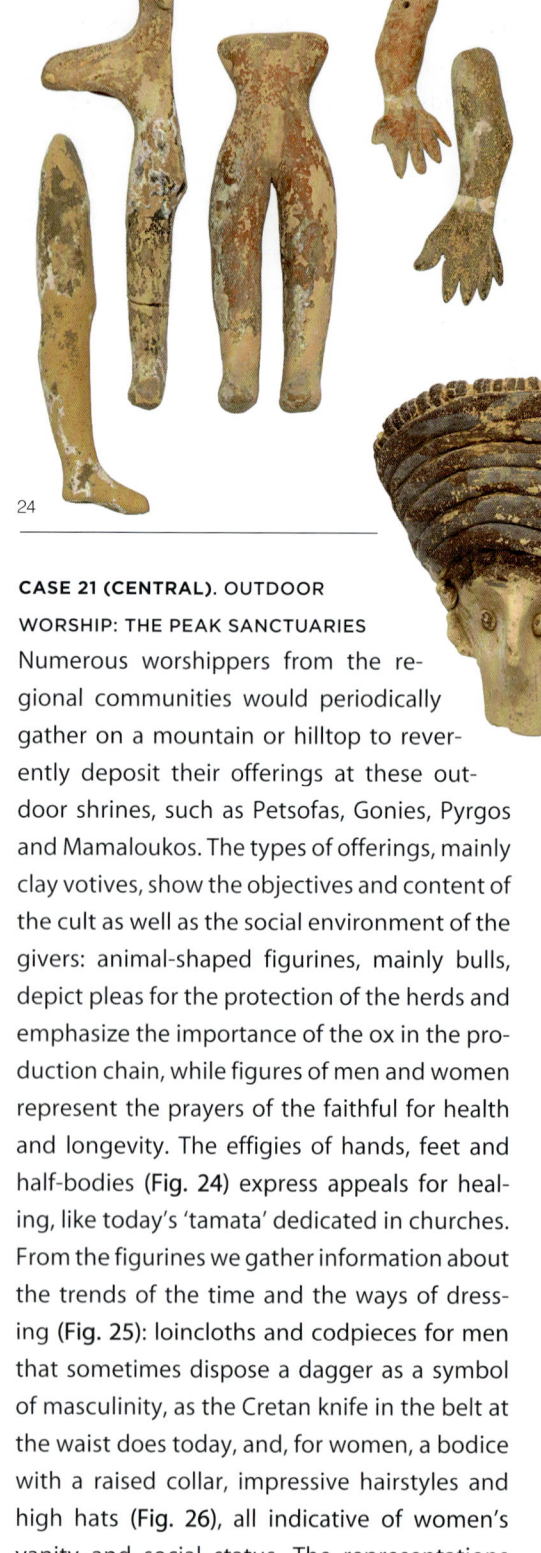

24

26

CASE 21 (CENTRAL). OUTDOOR WORSHIP: THE PEAK SANCTUARIES

Numerous worshippers from the regional communities would periodically gather on a mountain or hilltop to reverently deposit their offerings at these outdoor shrines, such as Petsofas, Gonies, Pyrgos and Mamaloukos. The types of offerings, mainly clay votives, show the objectives and content of the cult as well as the social environment of the givers: animal-shaped figurines, mainly bulls, depict pleas for the protection of the herds and emphasize the importance of the ox in the production chain, while figures of men and women represent the prayers of the faithful for health and longevity. The effigies of hands, feet and half-bodies (**Fig. 24**) express appeals for healing, like today's 'tamata' dedicated in churches. From the figurines we gather information about the trends of the time and the ways of dressing (**Fig. 25**): loincloths and codpieces for men that sometimes dispose a dagger as a symbol of masculinity, as the Cretan knife in the belt at the waist does today, and, for women, a bodice with a raised collar, impressive hairstyles and high hats (**Fig. 26**), all indicative of women's vanity and social status. The representations of buildings or rock formations where animals

25

climb, as well as enclosures, refer respectively to the urban environment and the mountainous landscape. The latter is where the devotees come from or live with their herds, and the enclosure represents the place of worship itself, shaped with rough constructions, and acting as a kind of fence defining boundaries.

CASE 22. THE WORSHIP OF THE DEAD
Aspects of the cult of the dead within a funerary environment are revealed by the offerings of anthropomorphic ritual-vases, mainly from tombs of Mochlos, Archanes and Malia (**Fig. 27**). These idiosyncratic vases in the shape of a female figure depict the patron goddess of the dead and were intended for the performance of libations – the ritual offering of liquids to the dead – since the vessels have handles and a spout for pouring out the liquid contents of the vessel. Animal-shaped rhyta and other double, distinctive tubular vessels for libations continue to be used. Two bull-shaped vessels from Koumasa (**Fig. 28**) and Porti in Mesara with human figures hanging from the animal's horns depict bull-leaping or bull-capturing scenes. Other bull-shaped figurine-rhyta from tombs testify to the performance of libation rituals.

An incised naked female figure with arms folded on the belly, outstretched legs and oversized pubic triangle is depicted on an interesting ewer, a type of jug, from an ossuary near the burial structure of Chrysolakkos of Malia,. She receives worship from two figures, perhaps the deceased. Although a simple enough scribbled sketch, the image graphically conveys the message of supplication to the goddess of the dead for rebirth in life.

The wall screen shows images of places of worship in the mountains, as well as finds from the excavations carried out at these sites.

24. Representations of human limbs and body parts, embodiments of appeals ('tamata') to secure healing. Petsofas, 1900-1700 BC
25. A couple of worshippers in a posture of prayer. Petsofas, 1900-1700 BC.
26. Figurine head with impressive tall hat. Filiorimos, Gonies, 1900-1700 BC.
27. Ritual anthropomorphic vase-rhyta for funeral libations. Malia, Fourni Archanes, Mochlos, 2200-1800 BC.
28. Rhyton in the shape of a bull with human figures hanging from its horns, representing bull-leaping or the capture of a bull. Koumasa, 2000-1800 BC.

ROOM III
Middle Bronze Age. Protopalatial Period (1900–1700 BC)

THE FIRST PALACES

The first palaces in Crete were built at the beginning of the Protopalatial period. They are large building complexes, of an intricate architectural structure, with central and western courtyards, theatral areas, ceremonial halls, storage areas and workshops. To date, four such building complexes have been partially excavated, under the massive later constructions of the new palaces, at Knossos, Phaistos, Malia and Petras in Sitia. A corresponding building at Monastiraki in Rethymnon is preserved in its entirety, as it was not covered by later buildings.

CASE 23. WRITING – ADMINISTRATION

A crucial factor for the organization of productive processes is the invention and implementation of writing systems for the documenting of goods and record keeping, as well as sealing systems for the certification of transactions. During the Protopalatial period, two writing systems were in use: hieroglyphic and Linear A. Letters or symbols act as syllables. In addition, logograms are deployed to indicate the types of goods traded in transactions whilst numerical designations measure the quantities involved. Clay tablets, rods, circular and crescent-shaped discs, as well as seals bearing hieroglyphic symbols, are used in this recording and sealing system. A unique example in the latter category is the bone seal with fourteen facets from Fourni in Archanes, bearing symbols of the hieroglyphic script: this is the earliest evidence of this writing in Crete (2000-1900 BC). The largest known set of sealings of the period comes from the palace of Phaistos and dates to the 18th century BC. They have the form of rounded lumps of clay with seal impressions, and were used to secure boxes or doorknobs. They bear complex decorative patterns with spirals and scrolls, animals and religious themes. The seals, usually prismatic, are three- or four-sided and made of soft stones: they were created in specialized workshops such as that of Malia. The seals made of hard, semi-precious stones (**Fig. 29**) make their first tentative appearance in this period. These seals, among a variety of geometrical themes, also depict human and animal figures with strong linearity and simple design. These representations clearly denote, in a dense and abstract manner, the specializations and professions (**Fig. 30**) of a complex social hierarchy. These are symbolic images, such as the ship (**Fig. 31**) which is a clear reference to navigation and the sailor's profession, while there are also depictions of the hunter, and the potter as well as vases, large and small, being the product of his skilled work.

29. Cornelian seal with hieroglyphic inscription. Malia, 1800-1700 BC.

30. One face of a three-sided seal depicting a fisherman holding a large fish. Malia, 1800-1700 BC.

31. Depiction of a sailing ship on a three-sided prismatic seal made of steatite. Malia, 1800-1700 BC.

32. The palace of Malia: central court, west wing and circular granaries.

MALIA

The second Minoan palace in north-central Crete after Knossos is located in Malia (Fig. 32): though larger than the palace at Phaistos, it employs less luxurious materials. The first palace was built at the beginning of the 2nd millennium BC and was destroyed around 1700 BC. The new palace was immediately built on its ruins; it was destroyed in 1450 BC, like the other palaces and most Minoan centres. Around the palace extend the quarters of the city, a part of which has been excavated. The complex burial structure at the 'Chrysolakkos' site with tombs containing precious items of jewellery dates to the time of the Protopalatial. The Museum's important exhibits from Malia include symbols of prestige and power of the lord, the ruling elite and palace officials (Rooms III, IV), as well as the famous golden bee-pendant (Room II). The initial investigations in Malia were carried out in 1915 by I. Hatzidakis, the first director of the Heraklion Museum, and were followed by excavations of the French Archaeological School, led by F. Chapoutier, J. Charbonnaux and P. Demargne who discovered the palace, the cemetery and quarters of the Minoan city.

32

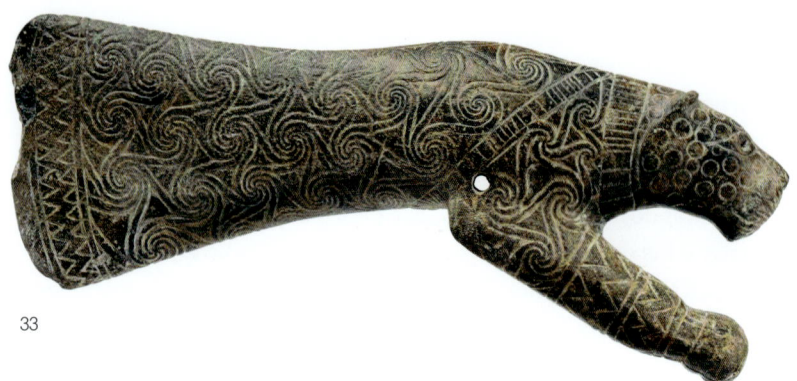

CASE 24. SYMBOLS OF AUTHORITY FROM MALIA

Symbols of power and office emanating from the top of the social hierarchy can be seen on the large luxurious swords and the smaller daggers with gold-plated handles found in the palace of Malia. Weapons of ceremonial function, such as the long sword with an ivory pommel and the large sword with a matching rock-crystal finial, display the wealth of the rulers, the prestige of office and the enforcement of power. A comparable symbolism resides in the stone sceptre whose axe-blade ends in a feline body (Fig. 33), thus combining two symbols of power and aggression. The wealth and glamour of the elite is mirrored in the bronze dagger covered by a gold sheared sheet running along the entire length of the handle (Fig. 34); it was recovered in a large building near the palace.

CASES 25, 26. RELIGION – CULT. VENERATION IN PALACES AND SETTLEMENTS

Places of worship and related material remains can be found in the urban fabric and the palace complexes. At the port of Knossos which was placed in Poros, Heraklion, bull and goat skulls were found in well-deposits, severed from the animals that were killed in hunting or ritually sacrificed. Perhaps the so-called bell-shaped figurines, actually models of horned ritual masks, were used in the course of these ceremonies, as denotes the faience example (also from Poros) with facial features drawn on it.

From the sanctuary of the Phaistos palace come tables of offering and kernoi, vessels with receptacles for offerings. In the same palace were found libation rhyta (Fig. 35) and vessels showing epiphanies, where the goddess or a priestess appears amidst groups of women dancing among plant patterns, which were symbols of fertility and flowering. A clay model of a palanquin from Knossos alludes to the way the ruler or priests were transported to great ceremonies, following Egyptian standards.

33. Handle of a stone sceptre in the form of a panther and an axe. Malia, 1800-1700 BC.

34. Bronze dagger whose handle has a gold, openwork sheath. Malia, 1800-1700 BC.

35. Rhyton for libations with a flower-shaped mouth. Phaistos, 1800-1700 BC.

36. The palace of Phaistos. A monumental staircase leads from the west court to the first floor.

PHAISTOS

The Minoan palace of Phaistos (Fig. 36), which, according to mythology, was the seat of Rhadamanthys, brother of Minos, was constructed at the beginning of the 2nd millennium BC in the Mesara plain. It was the powerful political and administrative centre of south-central Crete. Destroyed in 1650 BC, a new palace was erected later on its ruins around 1500 BC. This in turn was soon destroyed, around 1450 BC, without reaching the heights of splendour achieved by the previous one. From the storerooms and rooms of the first palace come hundreds of the famous vases in that unique decorative style, the polychrome Kamares ware; among them are the 'Royal Service' (Room III). Also, in the wider area of the first palace was discovered the famous clay inscribed Phaistos Disk with its yet untranslated hieroglyphic writing: it is the most enigmatic exhibit of the whole Museum (Room V). Precious jewellery and other expensive offerings dating to the next period, around 1400–1300 BC, have been found in tombs at the site of Kalyvia in the Phaistos area (Room X), excavated by St. Xanthoudides.

During historical times, in the 1st millennium BC, Phaistos was an important autonomous city that issued its own coins. It participated in the Trojan campaign, according to Homer, while Plutarch records it as the birthplace of the famous seer and theosophist Epimenides.

Phaistos was discovered in the early years of the last century, and was excavated by the Italian archaeologists F. Halbherr, L. Pernier and D. Levi. Their research is continued by the archaeologists of the Italian School of Archaeology.

36

CASES 27-31, 33-35. THE KAMARES VASES

The so-called Kamares vases come mainly from the palaces of Phaistos and Knossos and constitute a category of luxury pottery from specialized workshops. They were intended for the palatial banquets attended by distinguished participants. They were named after the area of these vases' initial discovery: namely a cult cave at Kamares, on the southern slopes of Mount Psiloritis. Patterns of white, red and orange on a black background form limitless combinations and compositions, dominated by the curve and the spiral. Most designs are purely decorative, however we can also see figurative subjects from nature such as flowers and plants (**Fig. 37, 38, 44**). Fauna subjects, such as fish between nets on a Phaistos jar, which foreshadow the naturalistic styles of the following period are rarer (**Fig. 41**). The Kamares vases figure among the topmost creations of prehistoric pottery in general; they are outstanding achievements of the Cretan approach to ceramic decoration in the mature Protopalatial period. A telling feature of the ingenuity, originality and boundless inspiration of the ceramic artists is the fact that,

38

37

despite the multitude of vessels of all known shapes and sizes, almost none is exactly like another. Along with pithoi and pitharakia (Fig. 42), amphorae and jugs, there are cups and bowls of all kinds and a teapot (Fig. 39, 40) with a strainer for preparing herbal tisanes. A group that stands out is represented by idiosyncratic vases shaped after a ship, animal or bird, but

39. Cups of various shapes with various polychrome decorations in the Kamares style. Phaistos, 1800-1700 BC.

40. 'Teapot' with a built-in strainer for preparing tisanes. Phaistos, 1800-1700 BC.

41. Kamares-style jar, with a rare figurative decoration of a fish caught in a net. Phaistos, 1800-1700 BC.

42. Pithoi with dense decorative compositions. Phaistos 1800-1700 BC.

37. Luxurious polychrome spouted vases for serving liquids, with complex decorative themes in the Kamares style. Phaistos, 1800-1700 BC.

38. Three large bowls with white decoration of foliate patterns and thysanos and tassels. Phaistos, 1800-1700 BC.

also vases for everyday use, such as sieves, trays, graters for juicing fruit and various strainers (**Fig. 43**). Numerous miniature vases (**Fig. 45**) were perhaps intended for small quantities of condiments or they were toys of the children living in the palace. An example of technical perfection can be witnessed in the so-called eggshell cups, with walls as thin as their namesake (**Fig. 46**).

43. Jugs, amphora, small askos and tray with polychrome Kamares-style decoration. Phaistos, 1800-1700 BC.

44. A kados (bucket) shaped Kamares vase with complex spiral-based floral decoration. Phaistos, 1800-1700 BC.

45

46

CASE 32. STONE VESSELS

The few and simple-shaped stone vessels contrast with the abundance and decorative diversity of the Kamares clay vessels, thus suggesting something of a decline in their production compared to the previous period. Among them, the limestone goblet service and a translucent alabaster cup from Phaistos stand out.

PEDESTAL BETWEEN ROOMS II-III. STORAGE IN PITHOI

Early palaces disposed large storage areas equipped with pithoi, such as the decorated medium-sized ones from Phaistos, in which foodstuffs, especially cereals and oil were stored (**Fig. 47-48**). The stockpiling of perishable foodstuffs was a key component in the chain of production and consumption for urban societies and for the palace elite. It ensured stability in the supply system, sufficiency of goods and the necessary surplus in order to organize large banquets, where the ornate Kamares pottery was ostentatiously displayed.

45. Tripod tray with miniature vases for seasonings, or children's toys. Phaistos, 1800-1700 BC.
46. Kamares cups, with walls as thin as an eggshell. Knossos and Phaistos, 1850-1700 BC.
47-48. Decorated storage pithoi. Phaistos, 1800-1700 BC.

47

48

CASE 35. THE ROYAL SERVICE

An apparent proclivity toward extreme decorative redundancy is exhibited by the four vessels of the 'Royal Service' from Phaistos (**Fig. 49-51**). It consists of a krater, a large fruit bowl, an ewer, and a stand (a clay cylinder for supporting a vessel). The 'Service' vases share compositions involving similar decorative patterns and serrated effects. They reach a striking climax with the large lily-like flowers rendered in full relief, that appear to grow straight from the crater's walls.

49-51. Luxurious palatial vessels: jug fruit bowl, prochous and krater, richly decorated in the Kamares style. They belong to the same banqueting set, a 'Royal Service', as shown by the similarity in some of their painted and relief decorative patterns. Phaistos, 1800-1700 BC.

ROOM IV

Late Bronze Age. The Neopalatial Period (1700–1450 BC)

THE NEW PALACES – THE ZENITH OF MINOAN CULTURE
After the destruction of the first palaces, probably by earthquakes, imposing buildings, known to us as the new palaces, covered the ruins of the old ones. These building complexes surpassed their ancestors both in size and luxury, with a central and western courtyard, around which the official apartments, sanctuaries, storerooms and workshops were arranged. The largest and most impressive in its construction is the palace of Knossos (**Fig. 52**), seat of the mythical king Minos according to ancient tradition. Other palaces were established at Phaistos, Malia and Galatas in central Crete, with Zakros and Petras in the east. The foundation of the new palaces marks the beginning of an era of great prosperity in Minoan Crete, an era of wealth and power, artistic creation and cultural expansion in the Aegean and the eastern Mediterranean.

52

KNOSSOS

Knossos is the oldest, longest-lived and most important archaeological site of Crete (Fig. 52). The first settlement, a small camp of huts, dates back to the 7th millennium BC. By the 3rd millennium BC this had developed into a major residential centre. In the same place, on top of the old deposits was erected at the beginning of the 2nd millennium BC the first Minoan palace, whose subsequent story covers the centuries. In the Neopalatial and Final Palatial periods, from 1650 to 1350/1300 BC, the palace of Knossos was the chief centre of power in Crete and, according to later generations, the seat of the mythical king of Crete, Minos. It is the largest, grandest and most luxurious Minoan monument, covering an area of 22,000 sq. m. Its design and construction epitomizes the technical achievements, innovations and refinements of Minoan architecture.

The imposing complex, which rose three to five stories high, is divided into wings with labyrinthine interior routes through stairwells, corridors and great halls, all set around the central courtyard. Access from the south and north was respectively through the majestic Southern Propylaia and through the North Entrance Passage with its elevated and colonnaded bastions (Fig. 53-54a). In the western wing,

53

52. The palace of Knossos. The wings of the complex extend around the central courtyard.

53. The northern entrance to the palace of Knossos with its raised bastions.

which turned an external façade onto the large western courtyard (Fig. 54b) and an internal one to the central courtyard, there were places of ritual, such as the 'Throne Room', while in the east wing were sited the 'Royal Apartments'. All this, together with the Theatral Area and the courtyards for public events, the luxurious halls for palatial gatherings, the storerooms with their huge pithoi, the workshops and the complex hydraulic and sewage network, created in one harmonious architectural composition the Knossian palace complex – a quintessential symbol of Minoan civilization.

It is from the luxurious furnishings and decoration of the palace and the surrounding Minoan buildings, such as the Little Palace, the South House, the 'Guest House', as well as from grave-goods from burial buildings and cemeteries, like the Temple Tomb, the warrior graves and similar that some of the most famous exhibits of the Museum originate. Among these are the Snake Goddesses, the bull's-head rhyton (Room VIII), the ivory bull-leaper (Room VI), the fresco of the 'Prince with the Lilies', 'La Parisienne' (Room XIII) and the Bull-Leaping scenes (Room VI), as well as valuable objects of jewellery, seals and weapons (Rooms IX, X). Similar and equally valuable finds come from the settlement and the cemetery at the harbour-town of Knossos in Poros-Katsambas, a modern suburb east of Heraklion (Rooms V and IX).

Knossos, however, did not disappear with the decline of the Creto-Mycenaean world. In early historical times, the Proto-geometric to Geometric periods, i.e. from the 10th century BC onwards, it is once again an important city in the region it influenced – the Knossian '*Chora*'. The wealth of this phase is reflected in the precious jewellery and ritual vases from tombs now exhibited in the Museum (Room XIX). Knossos was also operating during the Classical period, as sculptures from temples show (Room XXVI). During the Roman era, being a colony of settlers from Capua, it had mansions and public buildings with mosaics and statues (Room XXVII). Many finds from all periods at Knossos are exhibited in the halls of the Museum.

The first research in Knossos was carried out in 1878, by the antiquarian Minos Kalokairinos of Heraklion, who discovered the palace and excavated part of the storage area with the large pithoi. Subsequently, the palace, its peripheral buildings and large cemeteries were uncovered from 1900 on during the first decades of the previous century by the British in the person of Sir Arthur Evans, curator of the Ashmolean Museum, Oxford. He went on to lay the foundations of Minoan archaeology with his multivolume work *The Palace of Minos at Knossos*. Excavations continued for many years by the British School of Archaeology, while investigations are today undertaken in the area also by the Ephorate of Antiquities of Heraklion.

54 a

54 b

CASES 36, 37. AND A MODEL OF THE PALACE OF KNOSSOS. THE MINOAN WORLD – ARCHITECTURE

Complex architectural, morphological and constructional innovations were applied in the construction of palaces and large buildings in the cities and in the countryside. These include the use of large dressed blocks on the façades, as well as timber ties to enhance their stability, the cladding of surfaces with gypsum slabs and lime-plaster, the latter often with mural decoration, with the further incorporation of stone bordering reliefs and other decorative elements, which enhance the impression of quality and luxury. In addition, these monumental structures had arrangements of multiple-doors (polythyra/pier-and-door partitions) and internal

light-wells to provide adequate lighting, ventilation and circulation, a complex drainage system, multiple and successive colonnades, grand staircases and balconies for internal and external circulation. These lent views to the surrounding landscape, as well as the opportunity to witness the rituals in the courtyards.

The complexity and size of the Minoan architectural masterpiece, the labyrinthine palace of Knossos, whose ground plan exceeds 20,000 m2, is beautifully represented through a large modern wooden model.

CASE 37. Morphological elements of palace construction are evident in the stone decorative frieze (**Fig. 55**) from Knossos with the emblematic theme of opposingly set half-rosettes, which also carry a religious significance, and the stone column model from Zakros – this may have once divided a window opening and it now provides a faithful representation of the aspect of the wooden Minoan columns. From Knossos come a clay model of a colonnade where birds, as epiphany symbols, sit on the ends of the horizontal beams of the roof, as well as a model of the system of multiple windows that existed on the façade of the upper floors. The decorative wall painting with spirals also comes from Knossos. An image of a Minoan city is given in miniature by the 'Town Mosaic' (**Fig. 56**), composed of painted small faience plaques. They represent the façade of two-story buildings made of ashlar masonry, with doors, windows and projections on the roof denoting the cover for the stairwell to the roof – all details from the Minoan architecture on the upper floors of urban buildings which were lost in Crete. The reconstruction of the plaques of the 'Mosaic' renders in a concise manner the image of a Minoan city shown in perspective, accompanied by scenes of the countryside depicted on other plaques with animals, plants and people, as well as by images of the sea, with waves and swimmers, all capturing fleeting moments of everyday life around the city's urban core.

CASE 36 (CENTRAL). THE ARCHANES HOUSE

The clay model of a house found in Archanes and dated to 1700-1600 BC provides a three-dimensional image of a Minoan single-floor building. All the basic architectural and structural

54a, b. The north entrance and façade of the west wing of the palace of Knossos facing on to the central courtyard. Reconstructions by Piet de Jong.

55. Decorative stone frieze with opposing half-rosettes in relief. Palace of Knossos, 1450-1300 BC.

56. Plaquettes of faience with details painted in colour, perhaps inlays from a wooden panel, forming the image of a Minoan city with two-storied houses. Knossos, 1700-1600 BC.

57.

57. Clay model of a Minoan single-floor house, with roofed upper colonnade and balcony. Archanes, 1700-1600 BC.

58. Luxurious tall porphyry lamps with relief decorations. Knossos, 1600-1450 BC.

59. Stone jug with relief decoration that imitates a woven basket. Knossos, 1600-1500 BC.

60-61. Floral and marine-style vessels. Knossos, 1600-1450 BC.

62. The Draughtboard. Palatial board game made of precious materials, with four conical ivory pawns. Knossos, 1600-1500 BC.

58

features of small-scale urban architecture can be found here: an entrance with a side window, a perimeter corridor ending in a portico and a lightwell, a central room with a column and a window, as well as an ascending ramp to the covered veranda (**Fig. 57**). The isodomic construction system of the walls is indicated by horizontal and vertical incised lines, while the columns supporting the roof inside and the cylindrical ends of the horizontal beams that support the balcony are also portrayed. There stands a female figurine facing outwards, of which only the skirt survives.

CASES 38-40. KNOSSOS – THE PALACE EQUIPMENT
The wealth and luxury of the palace of Knossos is reflected in many objects found on its premises. They are products of specialized workshops established in and around the palace: elaborate stoneware, such as the porphyry lamps (**Fig. 58**), with various decorative reliefs of plants, and the stone jug with relief decoration imitating a pattern of weaved baskets (**Fig. 59**), the ritual rhyton for liquid offerings with its vertically grooved surface, the fragments of another vase with octopuses in relief and an archer. The bronze vessels comprise another such set. The special quality clay vessels are decorated in the style which is characteristic of the period, especially the floral (**Fig. 60**) and the marine patterns, with decorative compositions of unique decorative inspiration (**Fig. 61**). The repertoire of the floral style naturally comprises subjects to do with plants, such as reeds, lilies, ivy leaves, crocus flowers, papyrus and palms. For the marine style, it is the world of the sea that provides the patterns: octopuses, fish, seaweed, starfish-suns, corals and shellfish such as nautilus-argonauts and clams. Spirals, religious symbols, and various geometric patterns in endlessly repeating arrangements characterize other styles of the period, such as the 'geometric' and the alternating style.

CASE 39. THE DRAUGHTBOARD

The creative potential of the workshops of Knossos on miniature crafts is highlighted in the 'Draughtboard' or 'Royal Gaming Board', a large rectangular board game of luxurious quality – a possession of the elite **(Fig. 62)**. Similar items are known from Egypt and the East, but of lower quality and simpler construction. The case from Knossos was crafted using the inlay technique – with rods, plaques and other pieces in ivory, blue glass and rock-crystal, covered with gold and silver sheets. It has been suggested that the four large ivory cones that accompanied it are the playing pieces that would have occupied the four circles along one of the board's narrow sides.

63

65

64

CASE 41. THE PALACES OF PHAISTOS AND MALIA
Luxury vessels, similar to those in the palace of Knossos, have also been retrieved in the palaces of Phaistos and Malia. Those from Phaistos that stand out boast relief decorations of dolphins in a seascape and a wild goat (aigagros), as well as other marine style patterns (**Fig. 63**). An excellent example of the floral style is the jug (**Fig. 64**) decorated with thick reeds growing on a riverbank, a subject influenced by the landscape frescoes. A cup is decorated with the double axe and the 'sacral knot', which are both symbols with religious significance. A female figurine with her head slightly tilted may depict a dancer (**Fig. 65**). Some impressive finds from Malia include a bronze basin with a relief decoration and fragments of other vases representing a bull and a sprinting feline.

CASE 42. THE ARCHANES PALATIAL BUILDING. THE PALACE OF ZAKROS

A palatial building of luxurious construction, with a propylon, halls, storerooms and a courtyard, has been excavated in the town of Archanes, south of Knossos. Richly decorated vases have been discovered here, depicting palms, ivy and crocuses, as well as religious symbols such as double axes and sacral knots.

The palace of Zakros, on the south-eastern edge of Crete, contained a wealth of elaborately constructed vessels, which are included in the exhibition units pertaining to external relations of the island and, above all, to worship (Rooms V and VIII respectively). Here are displayed the clay (Fig. 67) and metal vessels, utensils and other equipment. One marine-style ewer features nautilus-argonauts swimming between what look like strips of netting, a conventional shorthand representation of the sea. It is the work of a specialized workshop to which are attributed two other similar examples (see Room IX). A marine-style composition– with sun-starfish, shell-tritons and the seabed – brings life to a rhyton (**Fig. 66**). The metalwork includes a sword with gilded rivets, a large bronze brazier, a type of portable hearth for heating the interior spaces, and bronze square decorative plaques with papyrus reliefs, decorations for doors or box lids. Other notable metal objects from Zakros include the rim of a copper lekanis with double axes, a small silver ladle for serving liquids, and a silver juglet decorated with gold bands.

63. Marine-style rhyton with nautilus-argonaut among rocks and seaweed. Phaistos, 1500-1450 BC.

64. Jug with a dense decoration of reeds, a notable example of the floral style. Phaistos, 1500-1450 BC.

65. Female figurine with elaborate hairstyle. The posture of the head and hands perhaps indicates a dance movement. Phaistos, 1700- 1600 BC.

66. Rhyton with marine-style decoration, consisting of sun-starfish, shells, seaweed and rocks. Zakros, 1500-1450 BC.

67. Large stirrup-jar with a decorative composition of spirals, consecutive arcs and other patterns. Zakros, 1600-1450 BC.

ROOM V
Late Bronze Age. The Neopalatial Period (1700–1450 BC)

SETTLEMENTS – PORTS – TRADE. THE SCRIPTS

PEDESTAL. NEOPALATIAL PIRIFORM JARS

These are ornate vessels serving a special purpose, of generally medium size and standardized shape, probably used in ceremonies and banquets of ostentatious consumption. Those from Zakros and Pseira **(Fig. 68-69)** in eastern Crete are decorated with spiral compositions, bucrania (bull's heads), double axes and floral themes. The large porphyry stone basin with an ivy-shaped spout found in Agia Triada, is also a luxury vessel.

CASES 44, 45. SETTLEMENTS – CENTRAL BUILDINGS – VILLAS OF CENTRAL CRETE

Buildings with palatial characteristics, as demonstrated by their architecture and contents, functioned as the seats of local lords. The most important finds (exhibited in Rooms V, VI, VII) come from the so-called 'Royal Villa' of Agia Triada in south-central Crete, which was the largest such building, showing extensive application of the palatial architectural tradition . Clay vases decorated with patterns from the palatial stylistic tradition are exhibited here, among which are two alabastra with marine style decoration and one jug with double axes and sacral knots.

From the 'Villa of Sklavokampos' in the foothills of Psiloritis, where an archive of sealings was found, come vessels and utensils, such as the jug with a dense composition of zig-zag bands. The seaside 'Megaron' at Nirou Hani east of Heraklion appears to have been the seat of an official with religious duties. The luxury of this construction is impressive, with the extensive use of gypsum for wall coverings, porticoes, polythyra and light-wells. Inside it were found oversized bronze double-axes (Room VI) and tripod altars of plaster with polychrome decoration, which

68-69. Jars decorated with bucrania, double-axes and floral patterns. Pseira and Zakros, 1500-1450 BC.

70. Marine-style rhyton with dolphins in a grid pattern denoting the sea. Pseira, 1500-1450 BC.

71. A small bucket (kados) with spout and marine-style decoration on including shells, seaweed and rocks. Nirou Hani, 1500-1450 BC.

72. Basket-shaped vase with double axes in bands and a kados-shaped vase with ivy and papyrus patterns. Pseira, 1500-1450 BC.

would have been used in cult rituals. Another object of interest is a small clay bucket (kados) **(Fig. 71)** decorated in the marine style.

The large Neopalatial 'Houses' of the semi-mountainous site at Tylissos, southwest of Heraklion – true mansions in terms of size and quality of construction – were probably the quarters of local lords who controlled the western regions of the territory of Knossos. Similarly to the structure at Nirou, the connection with the highest architectural standards of Knossos is evidenced by the excellent quality of the dressed masonry, the polythyra halls and the 'Lustral Basins', which were semi-subterranean rooms with possible cult use. Some finds which are typical of the type and range of banquet rituals are the huge bronze cauldrons for cooking large quantities of food at banquets (Room VI). Other important exhibits from Tylissos are bronze figurines (Room VII) and fragments of miniature frescoes (Room XIII). Here are also exhibited vases belonging to the floral style.

CASES 46-48. COASTAL SETTLEMENTS OF EASTERN CRETE. PORTS OF CENTRAL CRETE

Four port settlements of eastern Crete – at Gournia, Mochlos, Pseira and Palaikastro – give the impression of cities with their urban planning and large buildings. A telling feature of their affluence and wealth are the many ornate clay vessels, as well as bronze and stone vessels and utensils. The two major ports in central Crete were Poros in the north and Kommos in the south.

From Gournia, where a large and densely built settlement has been excavated, with streets and an open square as well as a central administration building, some rhyta and two strainer-vessels stand out, the latter being items for

the production of aromatic substances. From Mochlos, a rich port settlement established already since the Prepalatial period, come a large stone lamp and a bronze basin with spirals in relief. From the important Minoan settlement on the islet of Pseira we have fine vases with marine-style decoration and a basket-shaped vase with rows of double axes (**Fig. 70, 72**). We can also see a stone rhyton and 'communion cup' or chalice, which are ritual vessels, as well as stone lamps.

At Palaikastro, on the eastern edge of Crete, a large Minoan settlement developed, a true city with excellent quality buildings integrated into an organized urban plan with horizontal and vertical road arteries. Here were found excellent vases decorated with the floral (**Fig. 73**) and the marine styles (**Fig. 75**). Among them lies the wonderful flask (**Fig. 76**) with an octopus swimming in the deep, its wandering tentacles 'hugging' the entire surface of the vessel, among triton shells, rocks and seaweed. The vase is an excellent example of the naturalist approach, the work of a master potter-artist who created inspiring compositions employing patterns of the marine style. Other important objects are stone lamps, a triton-shaped rhyton, a kernos and a bucket-jar whose perforated wall is decorated with bucrania and double axes.

Ritual utensils are recognised in the two rhyta shaped after bull's heads from Mochlos and Palaikastro, as well as the two bull figurine-rhyta from Pseira. One of them (**Fig. 74**), its horns cut back, is decorated with a netted pattern on the body, a conventional way of portraying the actual net of ropes that captured the bull during a hunt in the great outdoors.

The two large port settlements in central Crete, on the north and south coasts, served respectively the large urban centres of Knossos, Phaistos and Agia Triada. A large settlement developed at Kommos, on the gulf of Mesara to the south, with a central building of imposing dimensions and excellent masonry. A vase portraying a series of octopuses is quite striking.

The excavations in the settlement of Poros, the port of Knossos in the suburb to the east of Heraklion yielded much evidence on the systematic import of raw materials through maritime trade and then on the organized production of various items by specialized workshops. Clay and stone moulds were used to produce cast jewellery. Semi-precious stones, such as agate, sard, amethyst, jasper, and rock crystal, were turned into jewellery and seals. Seals in various stages of manufacture were found in a seal-cutter's workshop. Evidence for metal-working comes also from the raw materials ready for the casting process: a copper ingot,

73. Two ornate rhyta, decorated with goats' heads in full relief, painted plants and crocus flowers, spirals and other patterns. Palaikastro, 1500-1450 BC.

a lead bun ingot and a compressed lead vessel ready for recycling; a clay bellow's nozzle reinforces this metal-working trend. Commercial activity is evidenced by lead and stone balance weights. Some houses here were decorated with frescoes – a sign of wealth and luxurious living standards. Of the surviving fragments, one depicts crocuses with their red-stamens from which saffron is produced, while others imitate woven wall tapestries with recurring patterns.

74. Ritual rhyta in the form of a bull. One has cut-away horns and a net pattern over the body, alluding to the wild animal's capture by net and its domestication. Pseira, 1500-1450 BC.

75. Rhyta decorated with compositions in the marine style. Palaikastro, 1500-1450 BC.

76. Marine-style flask with a wonderfully naturalistic rendering of a large octopus swimming among seaweed, rocks, shells and sea urchins. Palaikastro, 1500-1450 BC.

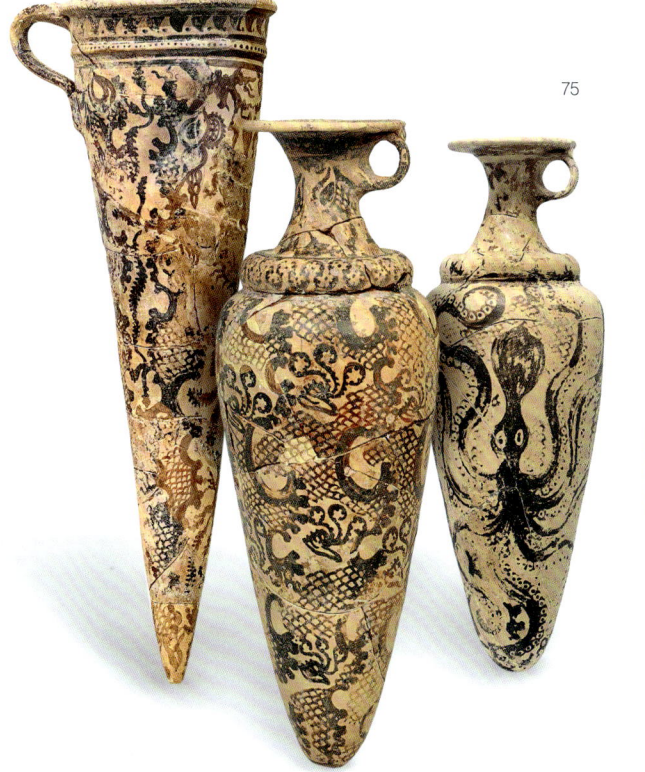

CASE 49. MINIATURE ART

Miniature masterpieces of Minoan art came from artists-creators producing small artefacts made of gold, ivory and semi-precious materials, as well as vitreous inlays fashioned in moulds. Their decorative themes are once more drawn from the world of land, sea and sky and their creatures, but also include sacred symbols such as the double axe and the sacral knot. Miniature works of special quality are to be seen in the two ivory figurines depicting children and the plaque depicting an exotic bird (**Fig. 77**) from Palaikastro and in two fragmentary compositions of ivory figurines from Knossos and Archanes. The minute gold pieces of jewellery in the form of a lion, a fish, a duck and a woman (**Fig. 78**) from Knossos and Gournia show exceptional delicacy. An excellent example of miniature painting composition depicting a bull-leaping scene, drawn with a very fine brush on a rock crystal plaque, comes from Knossos.

CASE 50. TRADE AND THE MINOAN THALASSOCRACY

The type, quality and origin of the imported raw materials and finished products alike demonstrate the extent and organization of the network of exchange conducted by maritime trade. The waves were never an obstacle for the Minoan seafarers. Quite to the contrary, the sea became their field of choice. Their ships reached ports and trading stations in the Aegean islands, Asia Minor, Egypt and the East, in places and countries where strong remains of Minoan presence have been found, ranging from station-facilities, through imported objects from Crete, to recognizable Minoan artistic influences on local products. Imported Egyptian stone vessels and utensils of alabaster and diorite were found at Knossos and in its port of Poros-Katsambas. Among them there exist an alabaster anthropomorphic vase in the form of a pregnant woman, an alabaster pyxis lid inscribed with the cartouche of the pharaoh

77. Ivory figurines of children and a plaque with a bird in relief. Palaikastro, 1500-1450 BC.

78. Minute pieces of gold jewellery in the form of a woman, a fish and a duck. Gournia and Knossos, 1600-1350 BC.

79. Gold-capped lapis lazuli seal cylinder of Eastern origin with depictions of demonic figures and symbols. Knossos, 1650-1450 BC.

80. Representation of a procession of Minoan gift bearers in an Egyptian tomb of the 15th c. BC. They are carrying artefacts of Minoan manufacture [© Metropolitan Museum, New York].

81. Stone relief anchor or standard-weight certification. Knossos, 1500-1400 BC.

Khyan of the Hyksos dynasty (second half of the 17th century BC) and a diorite statuette with a hieroglyphic inscription mentioning the official Uzer, a supervisor of goldsmiths (second half of the 17th century BC). From the East, commercial amphorae with their contents arrived at the Minoan ports: a Canaanite amphora at Poros, Syro-Palestinian and Cycladic mortars of trachyte, and obsidian from Asia Minor, used to make a rhyton from Tylissos. Elephant tusks were imported for the manufacture of ivory artefacts, such as one of possible Syrian origin from Zakros. Copper ingots of net weight of 30-35 kg imported from Cyprus were found at Agia Triada and Zakros. Their weight is approximately that of an earlier 'anchor' from Knossos: a conical porphyry object pierced for suspension is decorated with an octopus in relief (**Fig. 81**). It weighs about 29 kilograms, which is close to the weight of the ingot-talent; it could therefore be a device to certify the weight of imported copper ingots.

The seal cylinders are of Eastern origin, such as the gold-capped one (**Fig.79**) from Knossos, made of lapis lazuli, a material that comes exclusively from distant Afghanistan. From the islands of the Cyclades came to Crete a jug of unique shape, the so-called mastoprochous, with decorative nipples, as denoted by its name. From the Dodecanesian island of Giali (next to Nisyros) hails the large core of spotted obsidian: this material was used for vases like the triton-shell vase from Agia Triada, a *tour de force* of artistry and technique, as the stone is especially hard to work. Objects made of precious materials which required high skill were exported from Crete to the courts of foreign rulers. This is eloquently witnessed in the representation of a procession (**Fig. 80**) of the Keftiu, as the Egyptians called the Minoans, from the tomb of the palace official Rekhmire in Egyptian Thebes, which dates to the 15th century BC. The scene depicts Minoan envoys carrying objects of Minoan origin made of gold and precious materials, as their colouring shows: conical rhyta and vessels in the form of both a bull's and a lioness' head, are reminiscent of their counterparts from Knossos (Room VIII). They are clearly royal gifts offered by the Master hegemon of Crete to his counterpart, the Egyptian Pharaoh, in accordance with the practice of gift exchange that prevailed in eastern kingdoms.

82

83

CASES 52, 53 (CENTRAL). SCRIPTS AND SEALING PRACTICES

The reliability of commercial transactions was based on the development of systems for recording and measuring the types and quantities of traded products, as well as on systems to verify their weight and on sealed receipts for their certification and guarantee by the accountable authority. Small rectangular clay tablets and discs are used for the recording, and small lumps of fresh clay for the sealing. Words are succinctly recorded with incised syllabograms and logograms are used for the types of goods and merchandise , such as agricultural products, like wheat, figs, oil, olives and wine, but also animals, such as sheep, goats, cattle and pigs. Numbers and totals are recorded in detail with a decimal system, complete with fractions. The oldest script used is the Hieroglyphic, while the Linear A script (**Fig. 82**) gradually replaces it, being more specialized and functionally suited to the growing demands of the bureaucratic system. These scripts have not been deciphered, but the numbering system and logogram entries have been decoded.

The weighing process was carried out using scales with two copper discs that received the product and the weighing units. The weights themselves are stone or lead discs, as multiples or subdivisions of the basic weighing unit, calculated at about 60 grams. Writing is also used outside the context of commercial transactions, perhaps to render ritual phrases, poetic or dedicatory expressions, invocations and chants. Such Linear A inscriptions are incised on a gold ring (**Fig. 83**) from the cemetery at Mavrospilio at Knossos, on silver pins and on a series of ritual vessels. The use of ink for writing, possibly on papyri, is suggested by two cups from Knossos bearing inscriptions on their inner walls, perhaps magical incantations..

SEALS AND SEALINGS

During the Neopalatial period, seal-engraving reaches its apex in terms of artistic sensitivity and technical dexterity. At the same time, the large number of sealings, impressed by seals on clay balls, reflect the intensification of commercial activities and the organization of the bureaucratic system. The seals, made of semi-precious and other hard stones, bear engraved representations of the natural world of land and sea, religious symbols such as double axes, even bucrania and griffins (the mythical creature of eastern origin with the body of a lion and the head of an eagle). The portraits of figures of the ruling class or priests, such as those of the beardless youth and the bearded man from Knossos are rarer (**Fig. 84**). A series of seals with subjects portrayed and rendered in an abstract style are thought to possess a certain magical-prophylactic symbolism and were therefore called talismanic.

84

CASE 51 (CENTRAL). THE PHAISTOS DISC

The Phaistos Disc with its inscribed text, the most enigmatic Minoan object known, was found in 1908 in a room that was probably an annex of the northern wing of the palace of Phaistos. It dates to the beginning of the Neopalatial period, in the 17th century BC. The round clay disc, 16 cm in diameter, has figurative symbols imprinted on both sides in a spiral arrangement, running from the periphery into the centre. Forty-five separate patterns depict human figures and heads, animals, birds, fish, insects, ships, portable seats, ploughs and implements, skins and plant subjects. The symbols were impressed with small stamps while the clay was fresh and are grouped into 61 different combinations, separated by vertical incised lines, apparently dividing off words. The unknown script of the disc may be a variant of Cretan Hieroglyphic, but it is not related to the Hieroglyphic of the tablets. However, some similar symbols are recognized on a bronze double axe from Arkalochori (Room VII). Although many attempts have been made, the mysterious text has not been convincingly deciphered. Nor has the use of the disk, and its peculiar shape and arrangement, been fully appreciated. The text probably belongs to some poetic, perhaps religious, utterance: certain combinations of symbols are repeated and therefore appear to be a recurring exhortation or prayer (**Fig. 85**).

85

82. Clay tablet with an inscription in Linear A script. Malia, 1700-1600 BC

83. Gold ring with spiral inscription in Linear A, probably of religious content. Mavrospilio, Knossos, 1700-1600 BC.

84. Portraits of a bearded man and a beardless youth on a seal and on an impression respectively (representation in drawing). Knossos, 1600-1450 BC.

85. The enigmatic clay Phaistos Disc. On its two sides, 261 impressions comprising a total of 45 figurative symbols have been pressed into a spiral arrangement with small stamps. The inscription has not been deciphered, but the repetition of certain groups of signs in the form of a recurring pattern probably suggests that it is a hymn or magic-religious text. It is dated to 1700-1650 BC.

ROOM VI

Late Bronze Age. The Neopalatial Period (1700–1450 BC)

PRIVATE AND PUBLIC LIFE. BREAD AND SPECTACLES

Aspects of the private and public, non-religious, lives of the Minoans are best appreciated through the activities of daily life. These include food preparation, food storage, weaving, technical and craft work (such as items made from various materials), the preparation of such goods as wine and perfumes, as well as personal care for clothing and grooming. Public events and spectacles, like large banquets with numerous participants, in conjunction with the organization of sports' competitions and gymnastic demonstrations, fostered a climate of social cohesion, competition, participation and a sports-loving spirit among spectators.

CASE 54 AND PEDESTAL. DIET–STORAGE

Utensils, depictions and actual food remains yield information about the elements composing the Minoan diet, the ways of cooking and storing edible goods. A fresco from Knossos depicts olive branches, which produce the staple product of the Mediterranean diet, olive oil. A tub-shaped vessel is decorated with the plant and the fruits of the legume from which fava beans are produced. Food remnants from the household table include charred olives, figs **(Fig. 86)** and sea shellfish. Often, large quantities of animal bones are found in excavations, mainly those of sheep and goats, cattle and pigs, as well as of herbivorous wild animals and fish, which are a key source of protein and fat for the table of the wealthy classes in particular. Shallow and deep vessels, such as tripod cook-pots, were used for cooking over small hearths. We can also see the funnel a vessel

88

86, 87. Vessel with legume/fava-motif decoration, charred figs, tripod pots of various shapes and sizes, a tray for placing cups, a portable grill and 'spitted meat' stand. Various locations in central and eastern Crete, 1650-1450 BC.

88. Smoker for sedating bees during the collection of honey. Zakros, 1600-1500 BC.

89. Pithoi with relief decoration. Galatas, 1600-1450 BC.

for decanting liquids, whilst the grill and the barbeque-rest were used for cooking spitted meat (Fig. 87). To shuffle the fire and to place the food to be cooked, a pair of bronze tongs is used, which is identical to today's iron counterparts. Fishermen used bronze hooks of various sizes, and a smoker, a special pot with holes and a handle was used to pacify bees with smoke, as is still done today (Fig. 88). Images of everyday life, such as milking an animal, carrying the game home, and cooking in a tripod kettle, are depicted on three sealings.

Rich relief decorations embellish three pithoid-jars from the palace at Galatas (Fig. 89) and the 'Royal Villa' at Agia Triada that had been used to store agricultural products. They testify that jars of this type were not only utilitarian objects. As special, ornate and large-sized vessels, they would flamboyantly function as evidence of the wealth and affluence of their owner. Pithoi like these, but even larger and bearing a multitude of relief decorations, have been found in the palaces, mostly of Knossos.

CASES 55, 56. HOME HANDICRAFTS — CRAFTS — DAILY LIFE — PERSONAL CARE. THE NEEDS AND SMALL PLEASURES OF DAILY LIFE

The shape of many of bronze tools, hardly differing from their current counterparts, is telling of their use and specialization in the production economy. The pickaxe was used to dig the earth by farmers, chisels to carve stone by stonemasons, scrapers to work wood and leather, hammers, sledgehammers and double axes to break and chip stone or wood by quarrymen and carpenters, the drill to open up the stone for making vessels by the artisans, the huge copper saws to cut up the tree trunks by the lumberjacks, the querns and handstones to grind grain by the housewife and household personnel.

We enter the private world of the weaver when seeing the loomweights for stretching the warp threads on the loom, and the stone shuttle for passing the weft threads to and fro. The basic image of the upright Π-shaped loom with the threads hanging down is portrayed on a

89

stamped impression. In the spinning and working of the yarn, special utensils are involved, the '*dimititeis*' and the '*epinitron*' for unwinding the skein, as well as the wooden spindle, a tool for spinning and winding the yarn, of which only the weights (whorls) remain.

Household equipment also included stone and clay lamps for night-time light. The fuel was oil controlled by means of wicks, while the covered lantern with the light inside would have been useful for outdoors and for protecting the flame from gusts of wind. The potters' wheels, on which the clay vessels were shaped, bear witness to the activities of specialized pottery workshops. The basic system comprised two disks connected by a vertical shaft. The propulsive force was thus transferred by the potter's feet to the lower disc (a kick-wheel) and up the shaft to the top rotating disc. In this way, the skilful hands of the potter could pressure and shape the clay of the vase.

Special utensils were used for the production and burning of aromatic materials.

Board games offered enjoyment and fun: they were played with pawns and ankle-bones, a type of dice, and the board itself could be decorated with faience inlays, like the one from Tylissos.

Grooming the face and hair required combs, tweezers and razors for shaving, as well as round bronze mirrors with a polished reflective surface. The neck, hair, arms and wrists were adorned with rows of necklaces and bracelets. Toenails were sometimes painted red, as show fragments of frescoes from Knossos.

PEDESTAL. WINE PRODUCTION

The production and consumption of wine was a key sector of the economy, but also of religious and social life, as evidenced by the multitude of apposite vessels and drinking cups found in excavations. The grapes were crushed in large vats with a spout – the wine press. The must flowed into another vat, whence it was poured into jars for fermentation. Many installations were discovered, bearing similar features: either fixed in place, such as at the Vathypetro villa in the Archanes area, or mobile, such as the one exhibited from Tourtouloi, Sitia. The jar with an inscription of Linear A and with the wine ideogram comes from Epano Zakros (**Fig. 90**).

90. Movable winepress with a press and a vat for receiving the must, and a pithos with an incised ideogram of wine. Tourtouli, Epano Zakros, 1600-1450 BC.

91. The palace of Galatas.

GALATAS

At Galatas, Heraklion, in the hinterland of central Crete, a Minoan palace was discovered in the centre of an extensive settlement (Fig. 91). It was built around 1650 BC and destroyed by the great earthquake of 1500 BC. Following the typical design of palace buildings, the four wings surrounded a large central paved courtyard. The northern wing housed the official apartments, the seat of the local ruler. In the eastern wing is a pillared hall with a central hearth, perhaps a place for official gatherings and banquets, next to the palace kitchen. The excavation by the Ephorate of Antiquities of Heraklion, led by Giorgos Rethemiotakis, revealed evidence of the daily and religious activities in the palace and in the surrounding large houses of the officials: large jars, banqueting equipment and objects from places of worship, such as a clay model of a shrine with a seated goddess inside (Room VII).

91

CASES 57-59. PUBLIC LIFE AND SOCIAL EVENTS — BANQUETS — MUSIC

The large gatherings and banquets with the participation of the entire population became the arena for the demonstration of power and wealth by the leading class, who alone had the material means for their realization. Evidence of their size and the amount of food consumed at such banquets are the three huge bronze cauldrons from Tylissos (Fig. 93). Their repeated use is evidenced by the 'patches' of riveted plates where the metal had worn through.

Numerous clay cooking pots, along with serving and drinking vessels, were found stored in stacks in a rural mansion at Skinia in south-central Crete, testifying that the building also functioned as a large-scale banqueting centre for the local elite. Corresponding metal vessels of both high real and symbolic value come from Knossos (Fig. 92). A group of silver cups and

92. Bronze shallow plate with handle and bronze jug, banqueting utensils with relief decorations. Knossos, 1600-1450 BC.

93. Huge bronze cauldron for serving at banquets or communal feasts. Tylissos, 1600-1450 BC.

94. Large earthenware dish and banqueting utensils for serving food. Galatas, 1700-1600 BC.

95. Clay model of a circle dance, performed by a group of women and a female musician playing the lyre. Palaikastro, 1350 BC

96. Fragment of an alabaster lyre (and its drawn restoration). Knossos, 1500-1350 BC.

juglets from the 'South House' of Knossos is particularly interesting.

From the palace at Galatas comes a large number of banqueting utensils, such as cups, jugs, basins and shallow dishes, as well as large clay trays to transfer the dishes with food from the cooking galley to the banqueting halls (**Fig. 94**). A series of juglets and shallow serving dishes were also found in the coastal Minoan settlement at Agia Pelagia, west of Heraklion.

CASE 59. MUSIC.

The material remains from musical instruments, as well as the depictions of musicians, dancers and musical instruments, document the importance of music and dance in the Minoan community. Minoan musicians used wind instruments such as the triton-shell and the flute; also, they had a stringed one namely the lyre. Percussion, cymbals and the sistrum, a musical rattle of Egyptian origin, completed the ensemble. A characteristic case is the clay model of a circular dance of the Final Palatial period, discovered at Palaikastro (**Fig. 95**): here a group of women dance to the music of a lyre played by a female musician. A fragment of a real alabaster lyre in the form of a goose's head comes from Knossos (**Fig. 96**). The musician in the offering scene on the sarcophagus of Agia Triada holds an elaborate wooden seven-stringed lyre with a crescent-shaped soundbox and side-pieces holding the bar to which the strings are attached. They were also shaped in the form of a goose's neck and head. On the other side of the same sarcophagus, another musician with a Phrygian double-flute accompanies the sacrifice of the bull with music (Room XII). The handle of a bronze sistrum from Agia Triada has been restored and completed, based on a whole one found in Mochlos. Clay copies of sistrums have been found in Fourni at Archanes (Room II) and in the cave of Agios Charalambos in Lasithi. On the 'Harvester Vase' from Agia Triada (Room VII), a man is depicted singing to the rhythmical beat of the sistrum he holds high in his hand.

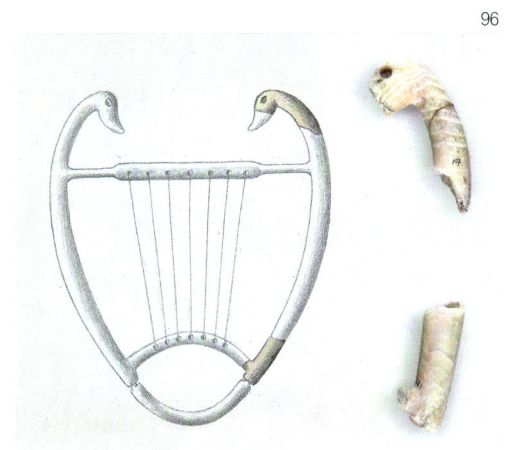

CASES 60-63. SPORTS – ATHLETES AND ACROBATS

Minoan communities developed and cultivated the athletic ideal of competition and excellence in sports with displays of skill, strength and endurance. The emblematic sport in Minoan Crete is bull-leaping, that jump over the bull's horns so dangerous for the athlete.

THE BULL-LEAPING FRESCO (FIG. 97).

The large rectangular panel depicts a moment in the bull-leaping event, the iconic Minoan sport in which the athlete performed a backflip over the horns and back of a bull running free in the arena. The scene of the jump here

97. The famous fresco of the bull-leaping. This spectacular Minoan sport is depicted here performed by a man and two women, with dark and white skin respectively. They perform the dangerous leap over the horns of a free-running bull. The iconography of bull-leaping directly alludes to the identity of the palace at Knossos. Knossos, 1600-1400 BC.

involves three figures, one man and two women: one young woman, white-skinned, holds the bull by the horns so that the male jumper, dark-skinned, can safely pass between them – he is shown in the midst of his backflip onto the back of the bull. The second female figure waits behind the bull with arms raised to steady the athlete as he lands. The dangerous and spectacular sport of bull-leaping is considered to be primarily associated with the palatial power of Knossos. This panel is part of a series, which were fragmentarily preserved and adorned a large hall in the eastern wing of the palace of Knossos; it dates to 1600-1400 BC.

97

CASE 61. BULL-LEAPING AND OTHER SPORTS

The sport of bull-leaping was particularly popular, as shown by a series of representations on seals, signet rings and frescoes at Knossos. It is related to hunting the bull in its natural habitat, as shown by the representation in relief on the ivory pyxis from Katsambas (**Fig. 98**), the port of Knossos. In this case, the hunt is combined with leaping above the animal's horns.

Running races were a sport taking place within a religious context, as evidenced by the representation on a gold ring from Symi Viannou: a priest stands in front of the approaching runner and a woman holds a worshipful position behind him (**Fig. 99**). Fragments of a fresco from Knossos seem to depict an armed race with the runners holding spears. Some of them are black, perhaps mercenaries, and are led by a Minoan, the 'Chief of the Blacks', who wears the typical Minoan belted loincloth.

Boxing is one of the tougher competitions, involving strength and technique. Fragments of relief frescoes from Knossos realistically depict scenes of bull-leaping and boxing with life-size figures. The intensity of the effort required is indicated by the way the tensed muscles are defined and the veins stand out in the athletes' arms and legs.

Acrobatics belong to the sports practiced to the enjoyment of a special audience in the palaces. The acrobat in relief on the gold sheath of the sword hilt (**Fig. 103**) from the Palace of Malia performs a full reverse bridge. Perhaps he was summersaulting over the upright sword, its point pointing upwards, in a veritable *salto mortale*, as the event was known in later sources.

Representations of chariots drawn by horses – perhaps moments in a race – are captured on sealings.

All the sports taking place in Minoan Crete, with the exception of bull-leaping, were included in the Olympic games and other major sports events of ancient Greece. In fact, according to

an ancient legend of Elis, the host city of the Olympic games, it was the Cretan Daktyloi from Ida, led by Hercules from Ida, who organized the first games and participated in the foot-race in the stadium, the only sport practised in the first games in Olympia. It thus appears that the mythic background of the games being set in Crete is supported by actual, archaeological evidence, showcasing Crete's pioneering role in the organization of sporting events.

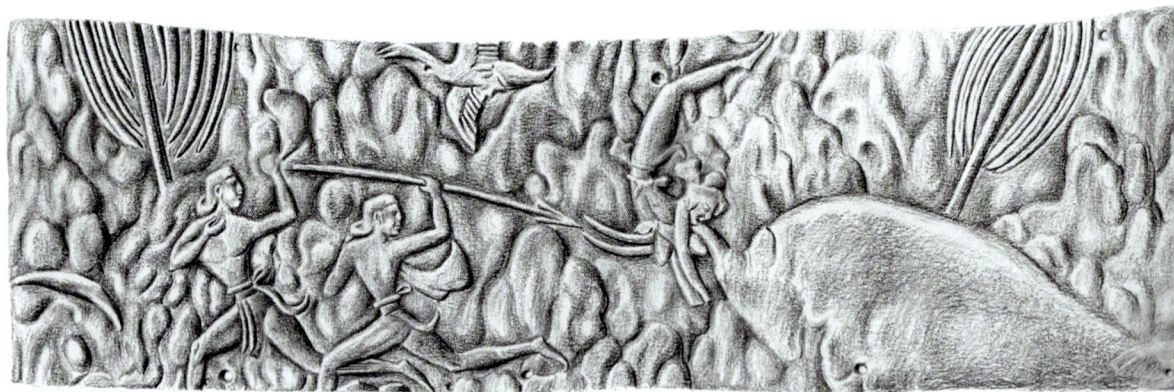

98. Ivory pyxis (jewellery case) with a relief representation of a wild bull hunt in a natural landscape, combined with bull-leaping. Below is a drawing of the scene. Katsambas, 1600-1450 BC.

99. Gold signet ring depicting a runner flanked by a priest and a woman in a worshipping posture. Symi Viannou, 1700-1450 BC.

100. The 'Sports-Rhyton' made from serpentinite. Relief scenes in a series of registers, cover its entire surface and depict scenes of bull-leaping and boxing. Agia Triada, 1600-1450 BC.

100

CASE 62. THE 'SPORTS RHYTON' (FIG. 100).

In Agia Triada was found a stone conical rhyton of ritual purpose made of serpentinite. It acquired this name because its surface disposes a series of registers in relief, showing the most spectacular Minoan competitive events, bull-leaping and boxing. The boxers are represented in pairs in front of colonnaded stoas reminiscent of those known in the palaces. The winner raises his arms in triumph over the loser, who is lying flat on the ground. The athletes wear protective helmets and boxing gloves as do modern boxers.

CASE 63. THE BULL-LEAPER (FIG. 101).

This is an elephant-ivory statuette, part of a three-dimensional composition of bull-leaping found at Knossos. It depicts the athlete at the moment he performs the dangerous jump over the bull. It is considered as the first surviving attempt in the history of art to render a three-dimensional form moving in space. The composition also included pieces of other bull-leapers, such as the fine portrait of an athlete (**Fig. 102**) who has a slight smirk on the otherwise calm face, thus expressing his self-confidence and determination.

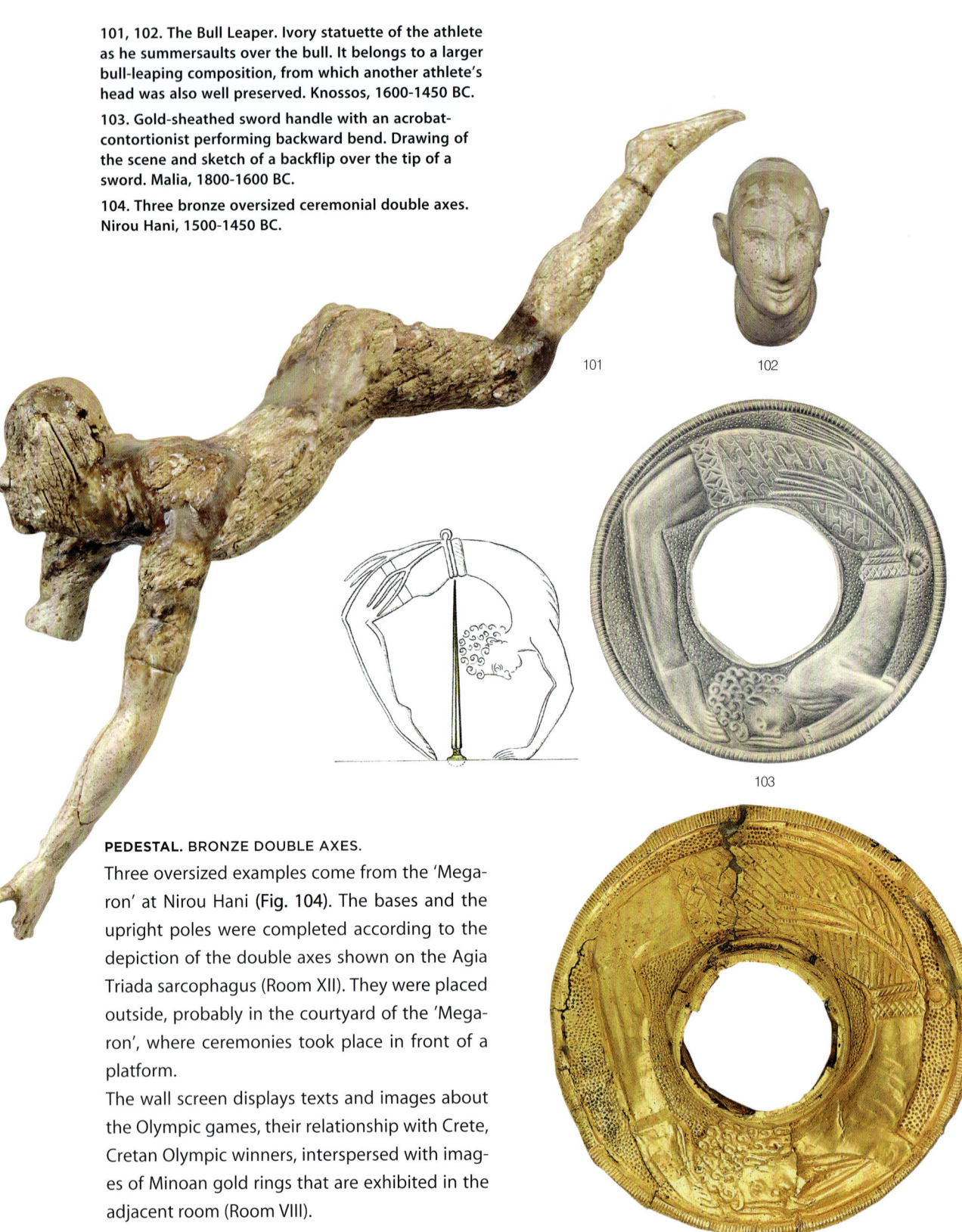

101, 102. The Bull Leaper. Ivory statuette of the athlete as he summersaults over the bull. It belongs to a larger bull-leaping composition, from which another athlete's head was also well preserved. Knossos, 1600-1450 BC.

103. Gold-sheathed sword handle with an acrobat-contortionist performing backward bend. Drawing of the scene and sketch of a backflip over the tip of a sword. Malia, 1800-1600 BC.

104. Three bronze oversized ceremonial double axes. Nirou Hani, 1500-1450 BC.

PEDESTAL. BRONZE DOUBLE AXES.

Three oversized examples come from the 'Megaron' at Nirou Hani (**Fig. 104**). The bases and the upright poles were completed according to the depiction of the double axes shown on the Agia Triada sarcophagus (Room XII). They were placed outside, probably in the courtyard of the 'Megaron', where ceremonies took place in front of a platform.

The wall screen displays texts and images about the Olympic games, their relationship with Crete, Cretan Olympic winners, interspersed with images of Minoan gold rings that are exhibited in the adjacent room (Room VIII).

ROOM VII
Late Bronze Age. The Neopalatial Period (1700–1450 BC)

MINOAN RELIGION. DOMESTIC AND OPEN-AIR CULT
During the Neopalatial period, small sanctuaries functioned in regional centres and in settlements, while worship continued also at mountain top sanctuaries and outdoor sanctuaries, but with several differences when compared to the previous period.

PEDESTAL. Horns of Consecration of poros limestone; these are a sacred symbol in Minoan religion, as is the double axe. They belong to the architectural crowning of an exterior wall at the Nirou Hani 'Megaron'.

CASES 64-66. ARKALOCHORI CAVE
The huge collection of metal objects from a small cave in Arkalochori in central Crete comprises a special and unparalleled case in Minoan religion, both in terms of number and type of dedications. Hundreds of bronze double axes of various sizes were recovered, among which some small ones of gold and silver stand out **(Fig. 105, 106)**. The ensemble includes many large and small replicas of swords and daggers, and copper ingots of plane-convex shape (bun ingots). Other categories of votives which are common in outdoor worship and one would expect to see are missing, such as figurines, offering tables and pottery. Given all this, the most likely interpretation for the situation is

105, 106. Votive gold double axes. Arkalochori cave, 1700-1500 BC.

106

that it represents an accumulation caused by the hoarding of valuable offerings from sanctuaries. Kept in the cave during a period of crisis, as is the case with the coin-hoards of later periods, they were never recovered, until discovered by chance in the early 20th century. The large number of replicas of swords of all sizes, none of which are real and functional, is particularly impressive: most are made of thin sheet and without a handle. Apparently, they were votives offered by a class of warriors who were ideologically linked with the value and symbolism of this weapon of warfare.

INSCRIBED DOUBLE AX

Besides the precious small axes made of gold and silver, one of the bronze ones has a hieroglyphic inscription in three columns and so is of interest. Some of the symbols bear similarities to certain patterns on the Phaistos Disc.

OPEN-AIR SANCTUARIES. THE PEAK SANCTUARIES

Worship in the countryside, on mountains and hills, is pursued during the Neopalatial period. In addition to the familiar categories of clay offerings seen in earlier, Protopalatial sanctuaries, namely figurines of people and animals, new votive offerings of a precious nature now emerge: bronze figurines, gold and bronze objects, stone offering tables, seals and jewellery, all representative of high social status and wealth of specific groups of believers.

JUKTAS

Mount Juktas, as seen from the northwest (Fig. 107). From here, its ridge resembles the profile of the head of a supine man: which relates to the myth that Zeus was buried here. On its mountainous mass, centuries of worship in outdoor sanctuaries and caves have been practised, from Minoan to Roman times. The ancient cult was followed by the Christian one from the Venetian period until today in the church of Sotiras (the Saviour) Christ on its southern peak, consolidating the reputation of Juktas as a 'Holy Mountain'.

107

CASE 67. THE PEAK SANCTUARY OF JUKTAS

On the highest peak of Mount Juktas, very close to Knossos, lies the largest and richest peak sanctuary in Crete. It has the form of a large built enclosure that hosts an altar-base, a cavernous chasm for depositing offerings and several auxiliary rooms.

The finds discovered in this site are representative of all the new categories of precious offerings: a miniature gold cup and a gold amulet (Fig. 108) with representations of a scorpion, an insect and a snake, apparently to ward off bites, bronze double axes, offering tables in a wide variety of stones and sizes, some with inscriptions in Linear A (Fig. 109), and stone kernoi with multiple cavities for offerings. Also of interest are bronze figurines and another of silver and lead alloy, dog effigies in various materials, numerous clay anthropomorphic figurines as well as animal and bird figurines.

CASE 68. THE PEAK SANCTUARY OF KOFINAS

The peak sanctuary of Kofinas, in southern Crete, at the base of the highest peak of the Asterousia mountain range, also had a small built enclosure with a rectangular niche. Some of the votive offerings that stand out are the large male figurines of up to 70-80 cm high, which realistically represent young men with an emphasized and muscular anatomy. Some are figurines of athletes, mainly boxers, their hands displaying boxing gloves, similar to those of the boxers in the 'Boxer Rhyton' from Agia Triada. Among the notable finds from the sanctuary, which appears to have been the most important of its type in southern Crete, is jewellery made of gold and semi-precious stones, seals, fragments of stone vessels and ingots of copper and lead, bronze figurines and dagger replicas.

THE PEAK SANCTUARY OF TRAOSTALOS

From the Traostalos sanctuary in eastern Crete, the figurine of a seated woman is of particular interest (**Fig. 110**) as she has a severely swollen leg. This is actually a material manifestation of an appeal to the gods for healing. Other offerings include a model boat, bronze figurines and gold bands.

CASE 69. OPEN-AIR SANCTUARY AT PISKOKEFALO IN SITIA

The sanctuary of Piskokephalo revealed a series of clay figurines of special quality. The soft handling of the torso, the realistic rendering of the robust legs of the male figurines and the impressive complex female hairstyles (**Fig. 111**) reflect the aesthetic standards of the time and of the devotees themselves (**Fig. 113**). Among

107. Mount Juktas from the northwest

108. Small gold amulet, with apotropaic symbols. Juktas, 1700-1450 BC.

109. Small alabaster cup, with an inscription in Linear A that probably conveys a religious utterance. Juktas, 1700-1450 BC.

110. Clay figurine of a woman with a severely bulging and swollen leg, dedicated to the shrine as an invocation for the healing of the ailing limb. Traostalos, 1700-1500 BC.

108

109

110

111

these figurines, the numbers, size and the detailed rendition of the *'copris hispanus"* beetles is truly impressive (**Fig. 112**). It is a type of scarab which certainly had some religious significance for the devotees. Two real insects of this species have been placed in the display case for comparative purposes. From the same sanctuary come clay models of buildings of dressed masonry rendered by incision and bearing horns of consecration – this evidence alludes to the connection of the worshipers with a nearby urban centre.

111. Clay female figurine heads with impressive high hairstyles, hats and headbands. Piskokefalo, 1650-1500 BC.

112. Clay figurines of a horned beetle of the species 'copris hispanus', one of which is carrying its young on its back. A specimen of the actual insect is pictured with them. Piskokefalo, 1650-1500 BC.

113. Pair of clay votive figurines in devotional postures, with a realistic representation of the male body and the female's dress and headdress. Piskokefalo, 1650-1500 BC.

112

113

CASE 70. DOMESTIC SHRINES. THE SANCTUARY AT ANEMOSPELIA IN ARCHANES

In a sanctuary with three rooms and a vestibule, located on the ancient road that connected Knossos with the sanctuary at the top of Juktas, an act of human sacrifice was performed, according to the excavators. A short spear-head decorated with an incised boar's head was used as the sacrificial weapon. The victim was a young man; the perpetrator was a priest who wore on his hand a fine quality seal (Fig. 114) of black and white agate depicting a rower on a boat and a ring of silver and an iron alloy, the latter being a rare metal for this time. A woman was also present in the scene. Their skeletons were found under the stones of the collapsed walls. Jars and many vessels were found in the other rooms, including a bucket with a relief representation of a white bull against a polychrome floral background (Fig. 115). A particularly interesting find are the

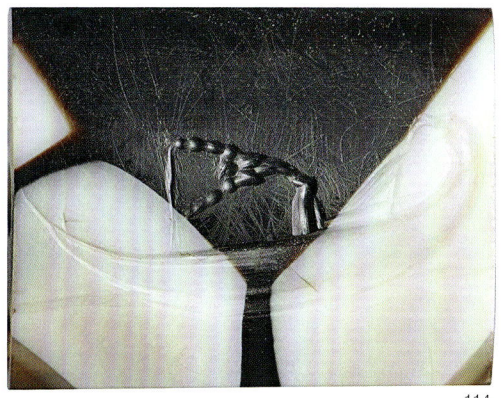

114

life-size clay feet of a large wooden idol of the *xoanon* type, which had been charred during the fire caused by the strong earthquake that destroyed the sanctuary.

114. Seal in the form of a flattened cylinder of agate, with a representation of a man bent forward and rowing a boat. Anemospilia Archanes, 1700-1600 BC.

115. Bucket with relief depiction of a bull in a landscape with vegetation, and its drawn restoration. Anemospilia Archanes, 1700-1600 BC.

115

116

117

118

CASES 71-73. DOMESTIC SHRINES. IDOLS AND UTENSILS FOR RITUAL LIBATIONS

Finds from domestic shrines at Agia Triada include many clay and bronze figurines who gesture in worhip, as well as the peculiar figure of the '*polymastos*' ('many-breasted') goddess (**Fig. 116**). Among them we see a seated figurine, perhaps depicting a goddess or priestess. From the 'Royal Villa' at Agia Triada come stone ceremonial vessels, rhyta and tall conical 'communion cups'/chalices, which received this conventional name because their use was thought to be analogous to the grail in Christian worship. A notable find is the conical stone 'Chieftain Cup' or 'Cup of the Report' (**Fig. 119**) of serpentinite, whose one side depicts two confronted male figures in relief, of which the older holds a sceptre and the younger one a sword on his shoulder with its scabbard. On the reverse, three men carry ox hides. The scene has been interpreted as a moment from a coming-of-age ritual for a youth: perhaps the young man is receiving the weapon from an officer or giving him a 'report' in a military fashion. The carrying of skins alludes to a previous sacrifice and the skinning of the animals alludes to a ceremony commemorating the event.

116. An unusual, headless female figurine with a dense pattern of knobs on the body. Agia Triada, 1600-1300 BC.

117. The 'Swing'. This depicts the epiphany scene, with the goddess descending from heaven, suspended between pillars. Agia Triada, 1500-1450 BC.

118. Clay model of the goddess or a priestess seated in a shrine. Galatas, 1700-1600 BC.

119. The 'Chieftan Cup' with a relief scene of an official with a sceptre or spear and a youth with a sword. Agia Triada, 1500-1450 BC.

120. Bronze figurine of a young man in a worshipping posture. He is shown wearing the Minoan belt and loincloth, and jewellery on his neck, hands and feet. Tylissos, 1600-1450 BC.

119

Another sanctuary at Kannia in Gortyna yielded figurines representing scenes of offerings and dancing. The offering ceremonies in sanctuaries involved the use of various types of ritual vessels, including conical and animal-shaped rhyta of clay and stone, libation jugs, stone offering tables, bases for double axes, ritual hammers, and tubular vessels used as vase supports and receptacles for offerings.

CLAY MODELS-RELIGIOUS IMAGES

Three-dimensional clay models are used to portray images of the epiphany, that is, the goddess's arrival and presence in the human world. Most come from Agia Triada. A case that stands out is the 'Swing', **(Fig. 117)** where a female seated figurine is suspended between two pillars on which are perched birds, symbols of the epiphany. This model depicts the hovering and descent of the goddess from heaven, the so-called visualized epiphany, as seen in depictions on golden signet rings. In a second model, a small column or baetyl is placed between pillars. It is the sacred stone that is the focus of ecstatic worship, another element also known from representations on rings (Room VIII). Birds, the symbols of the epiphany, both sit on the ground between the poles as well as on them. Other effigies depict male worshipers in a niche of a shrine topped with horns of consecration. A model from Galatas **(Fig. 118)** shows a goddess or priestess sitting inside her sacred house with her feet resting on a footstool, indicating her priestly status. The epiphany here takes on the characteristics of a dramatized episode, a type of theatrical event.

CASE 74 (CENTRAL). THE BRONZE FIGURINES

The worshipping postures of the Minoan figurines, especially the carefully crafted bronze ones, figuratively convey the spiritual condition of the believer at the moment of his communication with the deity. In the male figurines in particular, the strongly backward bend upper

120

torso, with one hand stretched down by the side and the other bent with the fist on the forehead in a gesture of supplication, underlines the intensity of the act. Two figurines from Tylissos are characteristic in this way, depicting a young man **(Fig. 120)** with a lithe frame and a mature man with a heavy, relaxed body in the same posture. Another figurine from Katsambas wears a tall conical hat, a symbol of priestly status. The female figurine with a long skirt from Agia Triada and the fine small male worshipping figures from the Skoteino cave stand out for their form and characteristic postures of worship. A special case, due to its large size, is the male devotee from Grivigla in Rethymnon.

AGIA TRIADA

Very close to Phaistos, at the site of Agia Triada was erected around 1550 BC the Minoan 'Royal Villa' (Fig. 121), which was destroyed in 1450 BC, like almost all Minoan centres. For a century though it functioned as the economic-administrative hub of the region after the destruction of Phaistos's first palace, and in so doing relegating the corresponding new palace to a secondary position. The complex consists of two wings with a courtyard in between, many rooms, official halls, storerooms and staircases. In the layer of destruction, finds of exceptional importance were discovered, which are prominent exhibits of the Museum: the 'Harvester Vase' and the 'Chieftain Cup' or 'Cup of the Report', bronze and clay figurines (Room VII), the 'Boxer Rhyton' (Room VI), the copper ingots from the coffer (Room V), clay sealings with interesting representations and tablets with the Linear A script (Room V), as well as wall paintings.

Later, around 1350/1300 BC, a Mycenaean megaron, the 'Agora', a sanctuary and other buildings where frescoes were found were built on the ruins of the destruction (Room XIII). An extremely important find of this period from a built tomb north of the 'Royal Villa' is the limestone decorated Agia Triada sarcophagus, with paintings from the cycle of the cult of the dead (Room XII). As in neighbouring Phaistos, the excavations of Agia Triada were carried out by the Italian Archaeological School.

121. Agia Triada: The formal hall of the "Royal Villa" with bases of the multiple doors at the entrance, a stone-paved floor, the surrounding built bench and walls covered by gypsum alabaster-type slabs.

122. The 'Harvester Vase' with a relief procession of marching men holding agricultural tools, singing to the rhythm of the sistrum and led by a man carrying a staff and wearing a priest's mantle. Agia Triada, 1500-1450 BC.

CASE 75 (CENTRAL). THE 'HARVESTER VASE'

(**Fig. 122**) The oval-shaped serpentinite stone rhyton was found in the 'Royal Villa' of Agia Triada and dates to 1450 BC. Its surviving upper part is decorated all around with a relief representation of a procession of men holding tools for reaping and threshing grain. One group is depicted singing loudly, their mouths wide open and chests heaving with the effort, accompanied by the rhythmic sound of the sistrum shaken by the reaper in front. The linear course of the procession is vividly broken up by the last group: a man has stumbled and is shown at a lower level than the others, while the leading man turns his head back to look. Both have their mouths open, as if reacting to the unexpected event. At the head of the procession is a mature man, holding a long staff and wearing a priestly garment, a sort of cloak. The scene has been interpreted as a procession of harvesters within the context of a rural celebration for the blessing of the new harvest by the deity. The 'Harvester Vase' is a masterpiece of the naturalistic style, a sample of the excellent artistic and technical quality of the Minoan stone-carving workshops.

122

126

of the trees that emerge from sacred buildings. Finally, the goddess is represented on a boat as a helmsman, sailing across the sea, which is indicated by an incised pattern of scales and defined by a coastline of massive rocks. The sacred boat with its seahorse-shaped bow carries a small shrine. The outstanding importance of the ring, justifying the conventional name given to it by Evans, has its evocative and excellent craftsmanship emphasized by its size and by the five rows of masterly granulation of three different sizes along the hoop (Fig. 127). Some elements are as yet without parallel in the small group of Minoan gold rings, although they are known from some Mycenaean ones. The 'Ring of Minos' is described as an accidental find in the 1920s at Knossos, near the palace, close by the Temple-Tomb. This eventful discovery was followed by an equally dramatic disappearance for decades. It was eventually handed over to the Museum in 2002 and presented as an exceptional exhibit, after its authenticity was first checked and confirmed in terms of iconography, style, manufacturing technique and metal alloy composition. It is dated to 1450-1400 BC. Along with the 'Ring of Minos', a series of other golden rings portraying both general representations and individual moments of the epiphany cycle are also exhibited. The ring of Mochlos, whose copy we can now admire, depicts the passage of the goddess across the sea in a boat carrying a sacred tree. On a ring from Kalyvia at Phaistos, the goddess sits in front of a column and is worshiped by a monkey. The ring from Sellopoulo at Knossos (Fig. 128) depicts an act of worship of a baetyl and tree by a male worshiper as well as a flying bird, which accompanies the goddess in her otherworldly appear-

127

ances. On a ring from Poros, an epiphany unfolds on two levels, with the goddess hovering inconspicuous and tiny in the background, but also seated between two birds. A dominant feature is the figure of the man-god on a pedestal, who 'converses' with the goddess by extending his hand to her. The composition is again completed by a tree-worshipping rerpesentation. In a ring from Fourni at Archanes (**Fig. 129**), the goddess is hovering in mid-air, dancing with a griffin, another ethereal companion on her journey, in a transcendent moment beyond the human senses. On another ring (**Fig. 130**) from the port of Knossos at Poros, a female figure is depicted in a posture of worship in front of a multi-storied palatial building with colonnades and a staircase, set on a hill with steps. The sanctity of the building is indicated by the consecration horns and a biconcave altar.

On a bronze ring from Gournia, the goddess hovers behind a tree, facing a female devotee. A ring from Kalyvia at Phaistos depicts the worship of a baetyl under a tree. In the ring with a complex scene from Fourni at Archanes (**Fig.**

126, 127. The gold 'Ring of Minos.' Scenes of epiphany and tree worship are depicted in the complex scene. Knossos, 1450-1400 BC.

128. Gold signet ring with representation of tree- and baetyl-worship. Sellopoulo, Knossos, 1400-1350 BC.

129. Gold signet ring with representation of floating goddess and griffin. Fourni Archanes, 1700-1450 BC.

130. Gold ring with a representation of a woman in a worshipping posture, facing an imposing sacred building. Poros, 1600-1450 BC.

131. Gold signet ring with a female divine figure between scenes of tree- and baetyl-worship. Fourni Archanes, 1600-1400 BC.

132. Gold signet ring depicting an epiphany and the ecstatic dance of women in a field with flowers. Isopata Knossos, 1600-1450 BC.

131), the central female figure, a priestess or goddess, is represented dancing between two scenes of worship of the baetyl and the sacred tree. Finally, a ring from Isopata near Knossos (**Fig. 132**) shows a group of women dancing and making gestures of invocation towards a central figure, perhaps the goddess. High in the background, a floating female figure on a small scale marks the visionary first stage of the epiphany. The religious representations on these rings are framed by symbols of cosmological and fertility significance, such as the Milky Way or a shooting star, sprouting fruits, flowers, insects and altars.

CASE 79. BULL'S-HEAD RHYTON

The bull was the sacred animal *par excellence* of the Minoan religion, a symbol of fertility and power. One of the leading creations of Minoan art is the serpentinite stone rhyton in the form of a bull's head found in the Little Palace of Knossos (**Fig. 133**). The faithful rendering of its natural model, with almost anatomical precision, is impressive. The right half is preserved, the neck and the lid behind it, while the rest and the horns are completed in keeping with a similar silver rhyton with gilded horns from Mycenae. The eye in the surviving part is also authentic: made of fine rock crystal and red jasper, while the muzzle is rendered in white mother-of-pearl. Next to the right ear and lid, there are some incised sketches in the shape of a bull's head. The libation fluid was channelled into the hole in the back of the neck, passed through the vessel, and flowed out of the muzzle.

133

CASE 80. THE SACRED SNAKE

Snakes constitute a symbol associated with the earth and they embody protective qualities. In a residence west of the palace of Knossos, inside a jar, were located effigies and utensils linked to the worship of the snake (Fig. 134): a clay model of a threefold and perforated honeycomb or 'honey pie' on which a snake lies coiled, holed juglets with attached snakes, peculiar tubular kernoi with cups for offerings and an offering table with four sections.

CASES 81-84. PALACE OF KNOSSOS – THE TEMPLE REPOSITORIES – THE SNAKE GODDESSES

The place of worship of the goddess in the palace of Knossos was the 'Central Sanctuary' in the western wing. After a disaster hit the palace around 1600 BC, objects from its contents were kept in vaults, from which they were retrieved during excavation. These include ritual vessels and related equipment, items portraying the forms and symbols of worship, vessels with offerings and sealings.

Worship in the 'Central Sanctuary' of Knossos seems to have focused around the Snake Goddesses, small figurines of polychrome faience carrying a strong religious symbolism and related to the Minoan mother-goddess of nature and the worship of the sacred snake. Two such figurines are best preserved, while fragments of others also exist. Snakes are coiled around the outstretched arms and torso of the larger figurine (Fig. 135); the head of one snake protrudes above her tall priestly hat. The smaller figurine (Fig. 136) also holds in her raised hands two small snakes, while the feline on her head denotes her dominion over wild nature. The goddesses wear richly decorated garments, an aproned skirt and a fitted bodice that accentuates their bare, fleshy breasts. Symbolisms are extended along the entire range of finds from the sanctuary: the sun-rosette made of rock crystal and the stone 'cross' are astral

134

133. The famous stone rhyton in the shape of a bull's head. Knossos, Little Palace, 1600-1450 BC.

134. Amphoriskos pierced with holes and honeycomb-'honey pie' with coiling snakes, models associated with serpent worship. Knossos, 1700-1600 BC.

bodies-symbols of the sky. On plaques made of coloured faience, the cow and the ibex (Fig. 137) nursing their young are depicted in a particularly realistic manner, constitute bucolic images inbued with symbolic expressions densely referring to the divine realm. . The earthly world of the goddess is completed by the addition of flora elements such as flowers, leaves and models of fruit in faience. The third aspect of the cosmos, after the sky and earth, is the sea, its animals and the seascapes of its depths: hundreds of natural oyster shells painted in vivid colours, as well as nautilus-argonauts, flying fish and rocks made of painted faience evoke patterns from the marine style in vase painting. Many other faience and fine crystal inlays would have adorned cult vessels. The functional ritual equipment of the sanctuary included the small faience vessels, such as the two cups with floral decoration, and the stone offering tables.

The painted faience plaques in the shape of dresses are replicas of actual garments dedicated at the sanctuary. Their decoration with saffron flowers alludes to the harvesting and offering of saffron to the goddess, as depicted in frescoes from Thera.

135

From the set of vessels for transporting products and liquid offerings to the sanctuary, two objects that stand out is the large jug from Melos with the representation of a bird and the Cycladic amphora with an inscription in Linear A (recording a quantity of 3,369 litres of wine sent by the Cyclades to the 'Central Sanctuary' of Knossos.

From the depictions on the sealings found in the sanctuary, a male divine figure stands out, a *'Potnios Theron'*, Master of Animals, walking next to a lion. On another sealing, a man on a boat is facing a sea monster – an image perhaps emanating from a Minoan myth.

135. Figurine of the 'Snake Goddess' from polychrome faience. She is depicted bare-breasted, in rich garments, while snakes coil around her outstretched arms and hat.

136. The second, smaller 'Snake Goddess' is depicted with long hair, bare-breasted, with a flowing skirt and a low hat. In her outstretched hands she holds snakes while a small feline sits on her head. Knossos, Temple Repositories, 1650-1550 BC.

CASES 85, 86. PALACE OF KNOSSOS – STONE CULT VESSELS

A series of ritual vases of various shapes made of alabaster and veined stones come from the palace of Knossos. Vessels such as these are depicted being ostentatiously carried by figures in frescoes that adorned the walls of palaces. A fragment of the Procession Fresco from Knossos is characteristic of this series: it preserves a hand of a male figure holding an amphora made of polychrome veined stone.

CASE 87. THE LIONESS (FIG. 138).

A rhyton, from the palace of Knossos acquires the form of a lioness's head, made from whitish translucent limestone. It is a masterpiece of plasticity and naturalism, clearly denoting the high skills of the Minoan artist-stoneworker. The inlays of the muzzle and eyes were not preserved, but were probably made of semi-precious materials, as in the bull's head rhyton, a piece of equivalent quality.

137. Painted faience plaque with a female ibex nursing her young. Knossos, Temple Repositories, 1650-1550 BC.

138. The 'Lioness', a rhyton made of limestone. The feline head is rendered with particular naturalistic fidelity. Knossos, 1600-1500 BC.

139. The palace and the Minoan settlement of Zakros.

ZAKROS

On the southeastern edge of Crete, beside a picturesque beach with a natural harbour, was founded in the 16th century BC the palace of Zakros (Fig. 139), in a position that ensured direct access to the trade sea routes of the East. It is located in a small valley cut across by a stream at the exit point of the impressive 'Gorge of the Dead', with its burial caves from the Prepalatial period.

The palace comprises official apartments in the east wing, workshops in the south wing, a kitchen, storerooms and a lustral basin in the north. In the larger, western wing with its ritual rooms and sanctuaries, the sacristy and treasuries of the palace were found intact in the layer of destruction caused by the fire of 1450 BC. The famous cult vessels from the treasury of the sanctuary and the valuable imported raw materials, such as copper ingots and elephant tusks, are among the important exhibits of the Museum. From a house near the palace comes sealings with most unusual representations of imaginary, daemonic beings, evidence of commercial activities and bureaucratic organization (all in Room VIII). Fine examples of floral and marine-style ceramics were also found at Zakros (Room IV). A stone pyxis with its lid handle in the shape of a recumbent dog comes from a burial cave in the 'Gorge of the Dead' (Room I). The palace of Zakros was discovered and excavated mainly in the 1960s by Nikolaos Platon, then director of the Archaeological Museum of Heraklion.

139

140 141 142

CASES 88-90. PALACE OF ZAKROS – THE TREASURY OF THE SANCTUARY

The largest ensemble of Minoan stone vessels of religious use was found almost intact in the treasury of the sanctuary in the palace of Zakros. Having achieved a high level of skill, the Minoan artist stoneworkers handled particularly hard stone in such a way that they were able to obtain an excellent decorative effect by exploiting the colours and veining of the stone. A typical example is the amphora with a double mouth (**Fig. 140**), S-shaped handles and red 'eye' in the centre of its body. Another revealing example of artistic and technical quality, given the difficulty of processing the particularly hard stone, is the 'communion cup'/chalice made of speckled Nisyros obsidian, a volcanic glass of a high degree of hardness that requires special work utensils, such as emery. Another famous case is the small elegant rhyton of fine rock crystal (**Fig. 141**) which carries at the junction of the neck with the body a ring of biconcave crystal beads, with ornamental gilt bone placers set between them, and having a handle of rock crystal spheres threaded on a copper wire. A thin-walled 'communion cup'/chalice of veined limestone has a fluted quatrefoil-shaped rim, another is decorated with dense horizontal grooves, while some rhyta have vertical grooves following the profile from the neck ring to the pointed tip.

The stoneware ensemble includes rhyta, open-conical or necked, conical 'communion cups'/chalices, zoomorphic rhyta, such as the specimen of serpentinite carved into the shape of a bull's head, libation rhyta and ritual hammers. We also see imported vessels, such as two Egyptian diorite vases reworked to adhere to preferred Minoan shapes, and other Egyptian alabaster vases. Raw materials such as copper ingots and elephant tusks, which are the raw material for making ivory objects, also come from the palace. Among the small objects recovered are a lifelike nautilus-argonaut model in greenish faience, small quadruple double-axes, and a butterfly (Fig. 142) in ivory. Some of the vessels were originally covered with a thin gold sheet to give the impression of solid gold. Traces of gold are preserved in the nostrils of an incomplete stone bull's-head rhyton and the important serpentinite rhyton portraying a peak sanctuary.

The Peak Sanctuary Rhyton, which has been preserved intact, bears over its entire surface a relief representation of a sanctuary with altars and an enclosure set in a mountainous landscape with ibexes (Fig. 143). The tripartite façade of the sanctuary dominates the back side of the enclosure, with the ibexes sitting in facing couples on the edges of the roof, acting as guardians of the baetyl, the sacred stone set in the centre between them. Birds fly over the consecration horns. Tall poles, attached to columns at the corners of the tripartite façade, may be flagpoles, like the corresponding ones that flanked the pylons in the great Egyptian temples.

140. Elaborate ritual amphora of veined stone. Zakros, 1500-1450 BC.

141. Small elegant rhyton of rock crystal. Zakros, 1500-1450 BC.

142. Small ivory butterfly. Zakros, 1500-1450 BC.

143. Stone relief 'Peak Sanctuary Rhyton', with traces of gold-leaf plating. It depicts a built shrine and temenos enclosure in a mountainous rocky landscape with ibexes and birds. Zakros, 1500-1450 BC.

144

CASE 91. RELIGIOUS SYMBOLS

The sacred symbols of Minoan religion, portrayed individually or included in figurative compositions, were recognizable by the faithful by symbolisms conveyed by their form.

Horns of consecration constitute one of two major religious symbols. Apart from the cases used as an architectural element in the decoration of buildings, there are also smaller clay and stone effigies such as those from Knossos and Poros. Sometimes they appear in figurative compositions, often in combination with the double axe, which is the second important religious symbol. The horns of consecration are thought to be a stylized version of the horns of the sacred animal, the bull, but they could also symbolize the 'cosmic horizon', according to Egyptian hieroglyphics.

The double axe is the instrument used to perform the bull sacrifice, though other researchers also interpret it as an astral symbol. Versions made of copper/bronze, gold and silver are valuable votive offerings in sanctuaries, such as the fourfold bronze specimen from the sanctuary of the palace of Zakros with its embossed and engraved decoration.

The 'sacral knot', a symbol with magical, prophylactic properties, may exist as an independent theme in a fresco, on a relief vase and as an ivory inlay, but it is also depicted on the neck of the female priestess figure in the 'La Parisienne' fresco (Room XIII). The 'sacred robe', a divine garment, is depicted on a bronze double axe combined with a sword. On a sealing it appears threaded onto a pole so it might be carried and displayed in a procession. The 'figure-of-eight shield' as an apotropaic symbol is included in sealing depictions, vase decoration and wall paintings. The 'biconcave altar' depicted in religious settings has the shape of real stone altars: it is too a religious symbol. The 'snake-like frame,' another sacred symbol, resembles a head cover with long, symmetrically fixed serpentine outgrowths: it is associated with the epiphany.

The relief representation on the fragment of a small ivory pyxis (jewellery box) from Agia Triada captures a vivid image of the festive decoration in a shrine , with women hanging garlands from the ends of masts set on platforms in the yard of a shrine. The 'Tri-columnar Shrine' (**Fig. 144**), a building of sacred character with three columns and sacred symbols, double axes and horns of consecration, is depicted in a fragment of a miniature fresco from Knossos.

CASE 92.

The long section of the 'Procession Fresco' comes from Knossos and dates to 1500-1400 BC. The dark brown legs of male figures in procession are preserved, converging towards a central female figure with white bare feet. The cosmic religious symbol of antithetic semi-rosettes on her skirt testifies to her priestly office.

144. The 'Tri-columnar Shrine', a fragment of a fresco depicting a building with religious symbols between and on top of columns. Knossos, 1700-1450 BC.
145. The Throne Room in the palace of Knossos. (Representation by E. Gillieron according to instructions of A. Evans)

ROOM IX

Late Bronze Age. The Final Palatial Period (1450–1300 BC)

**THE MONOPALATIAL SYSTEM OF KNOSSOS – A NEW DYNASTY.
THE FIRST GREEK SCRIPT**

After the destruction of the palaces and Minoan centres around 1450 BC, a new dynasty was established in Knossos, expanding its rule all over Crete. The new leaders, who have ties or descent from Mycenaean Greece, introduce the use of Linear B, the first script in the Greek language. New architectural construction programs are implemented with create impressive building complexes of the shipsheds or warehouses types in the two large ports of Poros in the north and Kommos in the south, while the settlement of Agia Triada in Mesara is also experiencing a new floruit now, as as it transitions into a main administrative centre.

145

CASES 93, 94. KNOSSOS PALACE AND HOUSES

The centre of secular and religious power in the palace of Knossos is the Throne Room. Here the squat alabastra stone vases were found on its floor during the excavation. These are unusual gypsum vessels with relief decorations that must have been used in a ritual just before the final destruction, between 1350 and 1300 BC. The painted representation of the Throne Room given by Evans (**Fig. 145**) shows the gypsum throne with benches around, the pictorial decoration of recumbent griffins on the walls and the alabastra on the paved floor.

Two sets of vases and utensils come from the Unexplored Mansion and the Little Palace, two large buildings of complex architectural structure in the settlement of this period at Knossos. The kylikes (**Fig. 146**), a new type of vase of Mycenaean origin, are decorated with stylized patterns of the floral and marine styles. From the Little Palace comes a ritual ewer with relief 'sacral knots' (**Fig. 147**) and a clay rhyton in the

146. Kylix with marine nautilus-argonaut pattern. Knossos, 1450-1400 BC.

147. Ritual jug with 'sacred knots' in relief and a vase with octopus decoration. Knossos, Little Palace, 1450-1400 BC.

148. Pithos and Palace-style jar, with decorative compositions of papyrus flowers. Knossos, 1450-1400 BC.

form of a bull's head. Evidence of trade activity via the sea routes is given by the trade amphora from southern Canaan and the stone anchor, with holes for fixing anchor stakes to the bottom, from Kommos.

BASES (LEFT AND RIGHT). STONE AND CLAY STORAGE VESSELS

The large stone vessels and utensils from Knossos are products of specialized stonework workshops and bear witness to the high standard of living of the leading class. Particularly impressive is the large, unfinished three-handled gypsum amphora from the 'the stonecutter's workshop' at Knossos. The magnificent clay Palace-style jars and pithoi (**Fig. 148**) from Knossos and Tylissos are also products of palatial pottery workshops. Decorative themes derived from land flora and sea fauna are included in compositions dominated by redundancy and decorativeness. They were intended for use at banquets of the palace elite as vessels of luxury and ostentatious display.

CASE 95. ECONOMY AND ADMINISTRATION – THE KNOSSOS ARCHIVE (LINEAR B SCRIPT)

In various parts of the palace of Knossos archival records were found inscribed on tablets and written in the Linear B script. They include records kept by groups of scribes that concerned goods and transactions. Their preservation is due to a fortuitous event: the clay of the tablets was baked by the fire that consumed the palace, and thus they were preserved within the layer of destruction. The decipherment of Linear B by the British Michael Ventris and John Chadwick revelaed that the script represents an ancient form of the Greek language. Despite the bureaucratic nature of the records, the texts contain an unexpected wealth of information. The records written over the course of time give important data on the collection and distribution of income by the central administration. Names of officials are mentioned, many of which are Greek, with titles of authority such as *(w)anax, basileus* – kingly titles (**Fig. 149**), but also political and social structures, such as *demos* (public assembly) and *asty* (urban centre). Evidence emerges on the levels of economic activity concerning both the rearing of large numbers of sheep for the production of wool, and the gathering of agricultural products, the artisanal organization of the production of wool and linen cloth, and the manufacture of aromatic substances for the needs of the ruling class, as well as for the export trade. A complementary role in the circulation of products was played by sealings on clay balls with short inscriptions that functioned as accompanying documents, a kind of receipt for transactions. Detailed records are kept of the equipment of an apparently numerous and heavily equipped army: swords and arrows, javelins, chariots and chariot parts, horses, helmets and armour. The names of gods of the Greek pantheon, such as Zeus, Poseidon, Ares, Hermes and Athena Potnia, are read in entries of offerings at sanctuaries (**Fig. 150**). The name of an important sanctuary, the Daedaleion, is recorded, an indirect reference to the existence of the mythical craftsman Daedalus; as well as the sanctuary of Eileithyia, goddess of childbirth and fertility in Amnisos, a port of Knossos. Priests and a priestess are also mentioned,: one of them bears the poetic cognomen 'priestess of the winds'. Finally, month names are found at the head of offering lists, indicating the existence of a religious menology. Apart from Knossos itself, the names of well-known later Greek cities and toponyms such as Amnisos, Sylamos, Tylissos, Lasynthos, Lyktos, Itanos, Phaistos, Kydonia, Syvrita and Aptera are listed as sites with activities related to the palace.

149. Large Linear B tablet with many lines, recording work groups under an official with the title 'basileus' ('king'). Knossos, 1425-1300 BC.

150. Linear B tablet with a record of offering amphorae with honey 'to all the gods' and to the 'potnia of the labyrinth'. Knossos, 1400-1300 BC.

149

150

Late Bronze Age. Neopalatial-period (1700–1450 BC)
CEMETERIES

CASES 96-98. The largest known cemetery of the Neopalatial period is in Poros, Heraklion, which was the settlement and port of Knossos. The tombs are underground chambers cut out of the bedrock, reaching a surface of up to 90 sq. m.. They had been used for dozens of burials from the Protopalatial period until the end of the Neopalatial period (1800–1450 BC). Similar tombs at Ai-Lias in Knossos were also used during the early Neopalatial period (1700–1600 BC). Of the vaulted tombs in Mesara, the monumental vaulted tomb in Kamilari is still functioning during this period, thus spanning a wide period of use from 1800 to 1300 BC.

The numerous vases from the tombs of Poros exemplify a range of styles: from the polychrome repertoire of the Protopalatial Kamares ware to patterns and compositions of the floral and marine styles of the Neopalatial period. A ewer of excellent quality stands out **(Fig. 151)**, a prime example of the decorative mannerism of the marine style in its mature phase: nautilus-argonauts swim on the seabed amongst a dense net of scales calligraphically painted with a fine brush, among seaweed, corals, relief trilobed features, rocks and clams. Similar, but less richly embellished in its motifs, is a ewer from Zakros (Room V), and yet another from Marseilles. All three apparently come from the same specialized workshop in the Knossos area. A cup with a cluster of crocuses **(Fig. 152)** is particularly noteworthy. In the tombs of Poros, a series of precious jewellery items of various types and materials were also found: among a host of finds, one can note four golden signet rings, relics from bronze weapons and utensils and also boar's tusks from helmet facings. This type of Homeric ceremonial helmet is generally considered Mycenaean. However, it is now proven that it had also existed in Crete during the Neopalatial period.

151

152

Many clay and stone vessels were found in the tomb at Kamilari. A clay alabastron stands out thanks to its dense composition of birds carrying in their beaks baskets full of crocus flowers. The somewhat poetic image is probably drawn from a narrative cycle linked to crocus harvesting, a version of which is also seen in the mural representation displaying monkeys engaged in the same activity (Room XIII).

The clay model groups from Kamilari dating to 1500–1450 BC are also important, in the sense that they represent rites of worship and offerings to the dead. One depicts a males' ritual dance (Fig. 153), conducted on a circular dance floor embellished with horns of consecration. Another group (Fig. 154) shows figures standing in a two-columned structure, depositing offerings on altars before larger-scale seated figures, perhaps their deified dead ancestors.

A third such group depicts a meal in honour of the deceased, with two seated figures and a table between them, while a third figure watches from the doorway. The sanctity of the occasion is underlined by the birds and horns of consecration that frame the scene.

PEDESTAL. BURIALS IN PITHOI AND LARNAKES

The dead in the tombs of Poros and Kamilari were placed on funeral beds, wooden biers or in coffins. At the same time, the older practice of burials in pithoi and jars continued elsewhere. The dead were folded up in a sitting (or foetal) position inside small jars, as is shown by a typical example of a burial jar from the Ai-Lias cemetery of Knossos (Fig. 155). Some burial jars from Knossos and Aitania are decorated with floral and geometric patterns. Others, from the cemeteries of Sphoungara and Mochlos in eastern Crete, bear richer decoration of papyrus flowers, octopuses and dolphins, the latter depicted at the moment of their synchronized leaping above the surface of the sea, a theme derived from the frescoes.

153

151. Elegant ewer densely decorated with painting and relief representations, eda superb example of the mature maritime style. Nautilus-argonauts are depicted swimming in a complex seabed landscape with additional shellfish in relief and tri-curved patterns. Poros, 1450 BC.

152. Cup with floral pattern decoration of flowering crocus plants, in a swirling arrangement. Poros, 1500-1450 BC.

153. Ritual dance of men on a circular dancing floor. Kamilari, 1500-1450 BC.

154. Model of deposition of offerings on altars before dead ancestors. Kamilari, 1600-1450 BC.

154

CASE 99 (CENTRAL). SEALS AND JEWELLERY FROM TOMBS

Neopalatial and Final Palatial period seals from tombs include outstanding examples of the art of Minoan seal engraving at its very peak. Their shapes are often lentoid, disk-shaped and amygdaloid, but three-sided prisms and compressed cylinders can also appear. They were often made from hard and semi-precious imported stones, such as agate, sard, amethyst, jasper, sardonyx, chalcedony and rock crystal. Only rarely were they made entirely of gold or with gold caps (around the suspension holes **Fig. 156**). Small tools such as various types of points, drills, chisels and tiny rotating wheels, as well as abrasive materials such as pumice and sundry lubricants were used to create the seals. Seal-carving workshops have been found at Knossos and Poros, with finds documenting the production process.

The images they carry are dominated by themes from nature: animals (**Fig. 157**) and birds, lions often attacking bulls (**Fig. 158**), as well as by daemonic and fantastic figures, such as the 'Cretan daemon' and the griffin. The daemon, who participates in libation offerings, takes the form of a predatory animal with a back cover resembling a tortoise shell and it is thought to be a variant of the Egyptian deity Tauret. The griffin has a feline body and the wings and beak of a bird of prey: it is a companion of the goddess as well as an all-powerful and aggressive monster. Rarely do we see religious scenes, such as *'Potnios Theron'* (the Master of Animals, a deity who tames wild nature), various versions of the epiphany, or religious symbols. A golden seal (**Fig. 159**) from Poros with a representation of a large dog, the guardian of the house, sitting on the garden fence is worthy of remark.

Many pieces of jewellery in gold, silver, semi-precious stones and faience, have been found in the cemeteries of the time, in Knos-

155

sos, Kamilari and, mostly, in Poros. Of these, a series of necklaces made up of beads of various shapes and colours (**Fig. 160**) stands out, as well as the rare specimen from Poros with amethyst beads and another one from Kamilari made of rock crystal and sard. Also found in the Poros tombs were gold rings with inlaid decorations (**Fig. 161**), silver pins, small gold plaques for suspension/attachment with reliefs of ducks among plants, and granulated gold earrings in the form of a bucranium.

155. Burial in pithos and ovoid larnax with spiral decoration. Knossos, 1700-1600 BC.

156, 157, 158. Gold-plated lapis lazuli seal depicting a man next to a lion. Sard seal with two bulls rendered in 'perspective'. Hematite seal with a scene of a lioness attacking a large animal. Knossos, 1450-1350 BC.

159. Gold lentoid seal, depicting a dog sitting on a garden enclosure. Poros, 1700-1600 BC.

160. Necklaces made of amethyst, gold, polychrome materials and semi-precious stones. Poros and Kamilari, 1600-1450/1300 BC.

161. Gold ring with decorative vitreous inlays. Poros, 1600-1450 BC.

ROOM X
Late Bronze Age. The Final Palatial Period (1450–1300 BC)

CEMETERIES. MONUMENTAL TOMBS – THE ILLUSTRIOUS DEAD
While the tombs of the Neopalatial period are relatively few, perhaps because the cemeteries of the palatial cities of that phase have not yet been found, in the Final Palatial period both the number of tombs and the richness of the offerings increase dramatically. The tombs are both of the chamber and vaulted/tholos types, but there are an additional three cases of imposing funerary monuments in the Knossos area, where members of the palace elite would have been buried. South of the palace lies the Temple-Tomb consisting of two burial rooms, an upper floor and a courtyard with a colonnade in front; north of the palace lies the Royal Tomb of Isopata, of large dimensions with a saddle-backed vault, and on the hill of Kefala is the large, Mycenaean type tholos tomb.

CASES 100, 101. KNOSSOS CEMETERIES
From the multitude of clay and stone vases in the tombs of Knossos, the so-called Palace-style jars stand out, as does a particularly important large set of imported Egyptian vases of the 18th Dynasty made of alabaster and porphyry, found in the tomb of Isopata, a valuable offering to distinguished deceased. The remarkable figurine (**Fig. 162**) from the cemetery at Mavrospilio, – like the later 'kourotrophos', the patron goddess of infants – depicts a divine female figure holding up a child in her arms, simultaneously symbolizing the renewal of life and its nurturing. Valuable offerings also included a silver cup with a gilt rim and a gold cup (**Fig. 163**) with embossed spiral decoration, which accompanied an early Final Palatial period warrior burial at Agios Ioannis, Knossos.

CASES 102-105. KNOSSOS CEMETERIES – THE WARRIOR GRAVES
In the tombs in the Knossos area, bronze weapons have been found in large numbers – swords, spears, arrows, daggers and knives, but also the helmets that accompanied warrior burials, as emblems of rank and office. They obviously belonged to a martial aristocracy, which corresponded to the elite that surrounded and supported the military power of the Mycenaean kingdoms of mainland Greece, as is shown by the luxurious and gold-plated weapons that accompanied the noble Mycenaean warriors to their final abode. Likewise, the Cretan examples of swords also had, in several cases, gilt-riveted and gold-plated handles, with engraved and embossed decorations and an agate (**Fig. 164**) or ivory pommel at the finial of the hilt. Such weapons were certainly not intended for use on the battlefield, but for display in prestigious

162

163

164

165

166

ceremonies. In tombs at the Venizeleio Hospital and Zafer Papoura at Knossos, helmets were also found, one of bronze and another covered with boar's tusks (Fig. 165), like the earlier examples from Poros (Room IX). The 'tusked helmet' of the Cretan hero Meriones, described by Homer in the *Iliad*, belonged to this type. Helmets are also depicted on a polychrome ritual vase from Isopata at Knossos (Fig. 166). The performance of ritual purification, through burnt offerings to the dead, is indicated by the recovery of a three-legged portable altar, with the coals still in place, in the tomb of the Tripod Hearth. Religious connotation is likewise added by placing bronze ritual double axes in the Tomb of the Double-Axes, whose name denotes the shape of the burial pit: a clear and emphatic statement of the priestly status of the interred person.

162. Figurine of the 'nursing/kourotrophos' type depicting a female figure holding up an infant in her arms. Knossos, 1450-1400 BC.

163. Gold cup with relief decoration of spirals. Knossos, 1450-1370 BC.

164. Luxurious ceremonial sword with gold-plated handle, decorated with an embossed and incised scene of lion hunting wild goats, and an agate handle finial resembling a mushroom. Knossos, 1450-1350 BC.

165. Helmet covered in boar tusks. Knossos, 1450-1300 BC.

166. Ritual polychrome vase with figure-of-eight handles and decorations of helmets and spirals. Knossos, 1450-1400 BC.

ARCHANES

According to Evans, the palace complex at Archanes, at the foot of the sacred Mount Juktas, was the summer residence of the kings of Knossos, which is ten kilometers away. This is a multi-storied building which revealed many decorated vases (Room IV). Like the other Minoan centres, it was destroyed by fire in 1450 BC.

Of particular importance is the large, organized Minoan cemetery on the Fourni hill, which functioned for more than a thousand years, from 2500 to 1350/1300 BC. The tombs are of various types: tholos (Fig. 167), built rectangular structures and a burial enclosure with pit graves. Burial deposits exist alongside ossuaries. Among the findings from the early periods are jewellery and Cycladic figurines (Room II), while from the later tholos tombs come gold signet rings (Room VIII), precious jewellery pieces and ivory artefacts (Room X).

The finds from the Minoan sanctuary at Anemospilia outside Archanes in the northern foothills of Juktas were interpreted as the remains of a human sacrifice (Room VII).

A large peak sanctuary, receiving numerous dedications, was also excavated on Mount Juktas (Place VII). The excavations at Archanes were mainly carried out by the Archaeological Society of Athens.

167

CASES 106, 107. KNOSSOS AND ARCHANES – THE GRAVES WITH BRONZES

The deposition of bronze vessels in sumptuous graves along with other valuable offerings signalled the high status of the deceased and their social class. Such sets were found mainly in the tholos tomb A and in the Mycenaean burial enclosure at Fourni Archanes, as well as in the Tomb of the Tripod Hearth in Knossos. The vases were primarily banqueting equipment, which would have been used in life for this purpose. Among them, one notes the bronze tripod cauldrons, the shallow tripod kettles, hydrias of various sizes, kraters, basins, ladles and lamps. A silver cup and an alabaster rhyton were also recovered from Archanes.

(PEDESTAL). HORSE SACRIFICE

In addition to the precious jewellery and many bronze vessels, the eminent woman buried in the side chamber to Tholos Tomb A at Fourni Archanes (Fig. 167) was honoured with the sacrifice and offering of both a bull and a small horse. The skull of the bull was found embedded in the entrance barrier towards the side burial-chamber, while the cut-marks on the skeleton of the horse, placed in the main chamber of the tomb, indicate that the animal was dismembered after it was killed and its pieces were arranged in a neat pile.

CASES 108, 109. CEMETERIES OF KATSAMBAS AND THE PHAISTOS AREA

The chamber tomb cemetery in the Katsambas area is located in the same area as the Neopalatial cemetery of Poros: it appears to have belonged to a social group connected to the palatial hierarchy of Knossos. The cemetery covers the period from 1450 to 1300 BC, meaning that it begins immediately after the abandonment of the former cemetery of Poros in 1450 BC. The vases are decorated according to the style of the time, with dense compositions of birds, fish and plants (Fig. 168) but also with

167. Tholos Tomb A at Fourni in Archanes, 1400-1300 BC.

168. Large jugs decorated with birds, fish and papyri. Katsambas, 1450-1350 BC.

168

169

171

boar's-tusk helmets with a plume , – this pattern bears strong semantic content, being an emblematic symbol of the warrior class.

Ceremonies for the cult of the dead are documented by finds such as two impressive ritual jugs (**Fig. 169**) with relief work imitating rivets of a metal original, censers with coals inside them for the burning of incense in acts of purification after burials, and a three-legged portable altar made of plaster. Stone weights for measuring small quantities of materials and Egyptian stone vessels could be alluding to commercial activity and the access that a deceased person would have had to the network of imported goods during his lifetime. Important finds are represented by the Egyptian alabaster amphora (**Fig. 170**) engraved with the cartouche of the pharaoh Thutmose III (1479-1425 BC) with the hieroglyphic inscription: 'The good god Men Heper Re, Thutmose beautiful in his transfigurations, gifted with life forever.' Before it was placed in the tomb, the amphora was probably among the royal gifts sent by the pharaoh to the ruler of Knossos.

In Phaistos, several bronze vessels similar to those of the cemeteries of Knossos and Archanes were found in chamber tombs with valuable offerings at the site of Kalyvia. Of particular interest are the rim and handles of a large bronze basin with a relief decoration of crocuses. A connection with Egypt, as in the tombs of Katsambas, is evidenced by the askos-shaped vessels made of Egyptian alabaster. The glass flask also comes from Egypt, but the elaborate triton-shell vessel of Cretan alabaster is the work of a Minoan workshop. The two clay askos-shaped alabastra (**Fig. 171**) are typical of this period: one is decorated with birds pecking at flowers and the other with a large bird that has grabbed a fish in its talons.

170

CASE 110 (CENTRAL). JEWELLERY AND OTHER VALUABLE FINDS IN GRAVES

Among other valuable gifts, rich burials also included numerous jewellery items, luxurious utensils and grooming tools made of gold, silver, ivory and semi-precious stones. The four large sets of jewellery from the cemeteries of Knossos, Archanes **(Fig. 172-173)**, Phaistos and Agia Triada reflect the wealth and affluence of the powerful classes. The necklaces made up of hundreds of golden beads in the shape of double-nautili, papyrus, ivy leaves, rosette-daisies are worthy of attention. Other neck ornaments are composed of beads of blue vitreous paste, faience and semi-precious stones: an impressive example being that of large beads of red sard from Phaistos **(Fig. 177, 179)**. From Knossos come earrings in the shape of bucrania **(Fig. 178)** with thick-set granulation and from the 'Tomba degli ori' or 'Tomb of Gold' at Agia Triada come golden amulet-pendants in the form of a bucranium and two lions. Another interesting find from the same tomb is the tiny drop-shaped gold amulet-pendant with apotropaic

169. Ritual jugs with rows of knobs. Katsambas, 1400-1350 BC.

170. Egyptian alabaster amphora with cartouche of Pharaoh Thutmose III. Katsambas, 1400-1350 BC.

171. Clay alabastra with compositions of birds. Phaistos, 1400-1300 BC.

172-173. Necklaces of gold and semi-precious stones and gold spiral hair clips. Archanes, 1400-1300 BC.

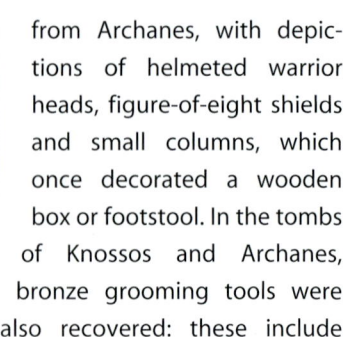

symbols attached: scorpion, spider, snake, a hand's palm and a spiral (**Fig. 175**). Some perishable precious material of amuletic value was probably contained in the two tiny gold boxes from Archanes. Gold rings with vitreous inlays were found at Phaistos and Knossos (**Fig. 176**) and others carrying depictions of religious symbols are known from Archanes.

Among the ivory artefacts, the mirror handle and plaques from Archanes with their animal reliefs, the mirror handle (**Fig. 174**) with a sphinx in relief and the distinctive ivory pyxides with their reliefs and inlaid decorations from Knossos are all exemplary pieces. Particularly important is the composition of relief ivory plaques from Archanes, with depictions of helmeted warrior heads, figure-of-eight shields and small columns, which once decorated a wooden box or footstool. In the tombs of Knossos and Archanes, bronze grooming tools were also recovered: these include mirror discs, some with ivory handles, bronze razors of various types and depilation tweezers. Minoan men are generally represented with clean shaves.

In addition to the valuable gifts and beauty accessories, other rare, 'exotic' objects were also deposited in the graves. The two stone vessels found in Agia Triada belong to this category: one in the form of a seated sphinx with a large cavity in the back, perhaps an inkwell or scented oil container, is of Hittite origin, while the second is made of alabaster, it is shaped as a female monkey and was an import from Egypt.

CASE 111. PERIPHERAL CEMETERIES

The end of the palatial era around 1350-1300 BC is also reflected in the contents of the tombs, the offerings of which become fewer and of lower quality than those of the previous richly endowed ones. Among the cases where the older traditions persist, albeit to a limited extent, is the cemetery at Agios Silas, where were found small and unadorned weapons, such as a short sword, and a few bronze vessels placed as burial offerings on biers. In most graves though weapons are now completely absent and the only goods are small clay vessels containing offerings.

174. Ivory mirror handle with a relief sphinx. Knossos, 1400-1300 BC.

175. Small golden amulet with apotropaic symbols in relief. Agia Triada, 1400-1300 BC.

176. Gold ring with cast vitreous inlays. Knossos, 1400-1300 BC.

177. Gold necklace with gold-capped sard seal. Knossos, 1400-1300 BC.

178. Earrings in the shape of bucrania. Knossos, 1400-1300 BC.

179. Four gold necklaces, a necklace of sard beads and a gold necklace with drop-shaped beads. Knossos, Phaistos and Agia Triada, 1400-1300 BC.

ROOM XI
Late Bronze Age. The Postpalatial Period (1300-1100 BC)

SETTLEMENTS. SANCTUARIES. TOMBS

After the collapse of the palatial system, various activities of daily and religious life became decentralized and were absorbed into the activities of small regional settlements. At the end of this period, when the gradual penetration of the Dorian races into the island begins, population movements to mountainous locations are observed, apparently due to insecurity. The centre of worship at a community level involves small sanctuaries that house figures of the deities with raised hands. Burials are usually poor, with but a few offerings.

180

CASES 112-114. POSTPALATIAL SETTLEMENTS

The ritual of large-scale and ostentatious banquets shifts in this period from the grand halls of palaces to buildings within the settlement. These often belong to the megaron type, with an elongated rectangular plan, anterooms and main areas with hearths, as well as storage and dining facilities. Workshop and household activities are revealed by the categories of objects found in settlements of this period: decorated vases and utensils of various uses, e.g. bronze needles, razors, spatulas and drills. Attention to personal grooming is evidenced by hairpins, tweezers and fibulae to fasten the tunic, the new type of garment. The complex of potters' workshops with kilns and potter's wheels at Gouves at Pediada demonstrates a pottery production unit organized on the community scale. From Palaikastro come clay figurines of birds (**Fig. 180**) and two interesting stone moulds for casting objects with religious implications: they depict cult and astral symbols as well as female figures holding flowers and double axes. A box-shaped earthenware vessel from Kastelli at Pediada depicts subjects from nature and an ibex hunted by a man and his dog.

CASES 115-118. THE COMMUNAL SHRINES

In the small communal sanctuaries, the goddess with upraised hands is dominant. The sanctuaries themselves are small rooms with built benches accross the entrance. The oldest sanctuary of this category is the Shrine of the Double Axes in the palace at Knossos, which dates to 1350–1300 BC. The figurines of the goddess and of her worshippers (**Fig. 181**) were found during excavation in situ, on the pedestal. The centre of the composition is dominated by the goddess – her arms are raised and a bird, a symbol of the epiphany, is perched on her head. She is flanked by two priestesses-worshippers turning towards her, while a male worshipper offers a bird. The composition is completed by stone horns of consecration, a plaster altar and vessels with offerings.

The following period is represented by the sanctuary at Kannia Gortyna, which dates to 1300-1250 BC. A notable feature is the increased size of the idols, a trend which will continue progressively in later shrines of this type, indicating the ever-increasing importance of the figures as the focus of worship. The sanctuary at Kannia is also dominated by the form and

181

symbolism of the serpent: snake heads in a row project above the toothed diadem of one goddess. In another the goddess is ostentatiously holding snakes, like the older snake goddesses of Knossos, while the bird, as the constant symbol of the epiphany, sits on her cheek. The set is completed by a male-worshipper figurine and a series of cult utensils of various shapes and sizes. From Gazi in north-central Crete and Karfi (Fig. 182-183) in the east come the next two sets of idols, dating to 1200-1100 BC. The figure of the goddess now overshadows all else completely: this is due mainly to its sheer size but also to the elimination of collateral elements, such as figurines of worshippers. The only element which is directly related to the deities in the place of worship are tubular vessels for receiving offerings and libations. Symbols of the divine aspects and epiphany, such as birds, sun-disc symbols, and double horns of consecration, are added directly onto the head of the goddess figurines.

THE POPPY GODDESS

The largest figurine from Gazi has behind her diadem what look like three stalks with spherical and incised heads. It is believed to depict the fruit of the poppy, the 'Papaver somniferum' poppy, from which opium is derived, the use of which soothes pain and brings relief to the ill. Metaphorically, it expresses the belief that the goddess protects man against pain and illness. An interesting clay vessel resembling a rhyton from Karfi succinctly represents a chariot with a rider, drawn by oxen. Cult vessels were also found in the settlement of Karfi, as well as in the sanctuary; they include a clay human-shaped rhyton, a clay slab ending in a head with human features, a basin with a figure with raised arms stuck to its inside and a clay perforated support for a vessel, with architectural features and religious symbols.

A similar shrine – a room with a bench, idols and vessels – served the religious needs of the Postpalatial settlement at Gournia in eastern Crete, dating to 1300–1200 BC. The finds include an intact figure and several fragments of goddess figures with snakes around the body and arms,

180. Figurines of birds. Palaikastro, 1350-1300 BC.
181. Figurines of goddess and worshippers. Knossos, Shrine of the Double Axes, 1350-1300 BC.

182.

182. Figurines of the goddess with Upraised Arms and with religious symbols on the head, such as horns of dedication. The largest, the Poppy Goddess, bears symbols in the shape of the seed-pods of the 'poppy of sleep' from which opium is produced, indicating the soothing anti-depressant and analgesic properties of the goddess' power. Gazi, 1200-1100 BC.

183. Figurines of the goddess with Upraised Arms and with religious symbols on the head, such as birds. Figurine of the bust of a rider in a three-wheeled chariot drawn by oxen, of which only the heads are represented. Karfi, 1200-1100 BC.

183

as well as tubular vessels, limestone horns of consecration, a plaster altar, a vessel stand and triton-shaped clay rhyta. Later still (1200-1100 BC) comes a set of figures and tubular vessels from Prinias in central Crete.

CASE 124 (CENTRAL). AGIA TRIADA–'THE COURT OF THE SANCTUARIES'

Alongside the covered sanctuaries of the Postpalatial period, other sanctuaries still functioned in open-air, thus continuing the centuries-old Minoan tradition of such worship. More representative, in terms of categories of its votive objects, is that of the 'Court of the Sanctuaries' at Agia Triada. In the area of the courtyard, in front of the ruins of the Minoan 'Royal Villa' and the Mycenaean Megaron, numerous offerings accumulated over six centuries of continuous use (1200-7th century BC). The numbers of clay and bronze anthropomorphic and animal figurines are huge. Two cast bronze figurines of realistic-looking goats and two bulls with decorative gold inlays on the forehead stand out. A quite original class is the group of clay figurines depicting hybrid 'creatures' (**Fig. 184**), having the body of a bull or cow but human heads and

184

feet. They represent daemonic figures, possibly bull-centaurs, or perhaps they echo theatrical mimes that took place in the Square with male warriors or hunters covered in ox hides. Horns of consecration with anthropomorphic features attached to them and small figurines of self-flagellating and cup-bearing men that have to do with Doric initiation rites were also discovered in this site.

CASE 125 (CENTRAL). UNIQUE EQUIPMENT FOR WORSHIPPING

This case displays typical examples of the nigh inexhaustible variety of religious vessels and votive offerings of the time. Most important among them are a clay rectangular panel-kernos with a series of attached juglets to receive multiple liquid offerings, a rhyton in the shape of a bearded head (**Fig. 185**), models of circular shrines, a small clay model of a sarcophagus-shaped tub with two seated figures inside facing each other, a pregnant figurine at the beginning of labour, a large head of a figure and a bull with painted decoration.

CASES 119-123. CEMETERIES - GRAVES - BURIAL PRACTICES

Compared to the richness of the tombs of the previous period, the contents of the Postpalatial burials reflect the decline in the standard of living and the weakening of the custom of

185

including objects and symbols that lauded the prestige of the deceased. Burials take place in chamber tombs, inside clay larnakes, though some earlier large tholos tombs are still in use, and new small versions are now constructed. Among the numerous vessels with simple geometrical, stylized or dense linear compositions, that now comprise the usual grave goods, clay censers (**Fig. 186**) for funerary purification rituals, often with coals inside them are of interest. We also see a tall conical rhyton for offering libations to the dead, a female figurine of the goddess-protector of the dead from Trapeza at Kalou and a peculiar ring-shaped vessel. *Pyxides* (cosmetic boxes) have also been found, some with their contents, as shown by the decorated examples containing the jewellery of the deceased from Trapeza at Kalou and another pyxis from Pachyammos with a bird decoration, which contained necklaces of glass beads of various shapes and simple gold rings-circlets. An unusual rhyton vessel in the shape of a boot comes from Karteros Heraklion and a large krater with a horseman and an ibex hunting scene from Mouliana in Sitia. A few weapons and bronze vessels testify to the continuation, as much as was possible, of funerary customs with gifts denoting class or office, drawing the necessary ideological sense from the glorious past.

A similar trend of continuity and connection with the prestige of the past, despite the meagre resources available, is indicated by the jewellery and grooming paraphernalia in the Postpalatial tombs, which were gifted to the beloved deceased. These are mostly necklaces made of cast glass-paste beads – cheaper substitutes for their gold and semi-precious counterparts of yore. A few gold rings, two with granulation (**Fig. 187**), maintain a long tradition yet preserved in some goldsmith's workshops. A gold rudimentary mask from Mouliana with the nose indicated in relief serves as a very distant memory of the gold masks from the royal tombs of Mycenae.

184. 'Bull-centaur', with the body of a bull and human head and legs. Agia Triada, 1200-1100 BC.

185. Rhyton in the form of a bearded head. Phaistos, 1300-1200 BC.

186. Censers with lid. Karteros and Klima, 1370-1300 BC.

187. Ring with granulation. Praisos, 1200-1100 BC.

ROOM XII
Late Bronze Age – Postpalatial Period (1300–1100 BC)

LARNAKES – THE WORLD OF THE DEAD

Clay larnakes or sarcophagi were used as coffins for the burial of the dead as early as the Prepalatial period. In contrast to the ellipsoidal-shaped urns of the Prepalatial and Protopalatial periods, in the Postpalatial times two main types can be distinguished – the rectangular box-shaped ones with gable, saddle or flat covers and the bath-shaped ones that indeed look like bathtubs. The deceased is buried in a contracted position with folded legs, the so-called 'foetal position', as shown by the skeleton inside one case from Tylissos. The scenes unfolding on the larnakes, with plants, land and sea animals, imaginary beings, human figures but also religious symbols, are considered to be related to metaphysical concepts and symbolisms connected todeath.

CASE 127 (CENTRAL). THE AGIA TRIADA SARCOPHAGUS

Unique in its material, the manner of construction and decoration, its representations and their symbolic 'narrative' is the larnax from Agia Triada (**Fig. 188**). It was found in a built rectangular tomb north of the 'Royal Villa' and dates to 1370–1300 BC. It is the only stone sarcophagus (made of poros limestone) known and its surface is covered with white plaster, on which were painted scenes from the cycle of the worship of the dead, using the fresco technique.

To the right of one of the long sides (**Fig. 189**) is depicted a male figure that appears to be emerging from the ground – and therefore is probably the deceased – wrapped in a full-length leather cloak. He stands between a stepped altar with a tree and a decorated building, perhaps

188

188. The Agia Triada sarcophagus with scenes of worshipping the deceased, 1370-1300 BC.

189. Funerary offerings and ritual libations in honour of the deceased, who is depicted directly in front of a building and wrapped in a cloak. The scene is conducted by priests and priestesses, accompanied by a musician playing the lyre. Religious symbols, double axes and birds underline the sanctity of the scene. First long side of the Agia Triada sarcophagus.

190. Sacrifice of a bull, tied to a table, with its blood flowing into a bucket. Priestesses and a musician flank the scene which is completed, to the right, with bloodless offerings made by a priestess on an altar in front of a small shrine topped with horns of consecration and a pole crowned with religious symbols, horns of consecration and a double axe. Part of the second long side of the Agia Triada sarcophagus.

his own tomb, and receives gifts from priests dressed in similar leather gear: a boat, symbolizing the deceased's impending journey to the paradise beyond, and two calves, offerings for sacrifice. To the left, two priestesses moving in the opposite direction pour liquid offerings into a vat between poles supporting double axes, the Minoan religious symbol. Birds are perched on them, as symbols of the epiphany. Behind the priestesses, a male musician in a long robe plays an elaborate seven-stringed lyre, accompanying the liquid libations with music.

On the other long side, four priestesses and another musician playing the double-flute partake in the ceremony of a bull sacrifice (**Fig. 190**), the supreme offering to the illustrious dead. The bull is tied onto a table and has already been sacrificed, blood is flowing from its neck into a bucket, while below the table two rams calmly await their turn. The last part of the scene is a double bloodless offering on an altar by a priestess in a leather skirt: a pannier with round objects, probably bread, and a libation ewer with its liquid contents. In front, there is a double axe on a pole and the epiphany bird sitting on it, as well as a small built shrine with a tree inside.

Two otherworldly scenes are depicted on the narrow sides of the sarcophagus, representing the imagined contribution of the gods to the funerary ritual for the ruler. On one side (**Fig. 191**), a chariot drawn by griffins carries two female deities in priestly robes and crowns. The metaphysical dimension of the image is enhanced by an unearthly bird with a crest. On the other narrow side (**Fig. 192**), a second chariot, drawn by two hybrid imaginary beings with a horse's body and horns, also carries two goddesses. In the upper register, a procession of men parade, perhaps in honour of the deceased. The whole composition illustrates the transcendent meeting of dead, living and otherworldly beings in the context of ceremonies to bid farewell to the deceased leader, departing for his afterlife.

191, 192. Otherworldly scenes with goddesses in chariots drawn by imaginary creatures. Narrow ends of the Agia Triada sarcophagus.

193. Larnax decorated with birds, papyri and fish, symbolizing a paradisiac landscape. Vasilika Anogeia, 1300-1200 BC.

THE REPERTORY OF THE FIGURATIVE CLAY LARNAKES

The metaphysical dimension of the Other Life, that comes after man's physical ending, permeates the entire iconography of the clay larnakes. The otherworldly landscape of eternal spring is symbolized by the trees and plants, birds and animals that cover the sides of the larnakes in images with layers of meaning (**Fig. 193, 195**). The animals of the sea suggest the element of water, the mythical Ocean, beyond which stretch the Elysian fields and the islands of the blessed dead, according to Homeric tradition. Griffins, double axes, horns of consecration and divine figures in abstract compositions with a strong symbolic content emphasize the religious dimension of perceptions of life after death. The compositions are loose, without any sense of real space, and the subjects are painted without great care, often in a mood of decorative overstatement.

CLAY LARNAKES

Important information about the content of this thematic cycle is provided by a series of larnakes with pictorial compositions of particular importance. The larnax from Gazi (**Fig. 196**) shows a sailing ship, with a rudder behind and a beak in front, swiftly crossing the sea as shown by the spirals, representing the foamy waves that 'burst' on the bow. It is the funeral ship, the means of transporting the deceased to the overseas islands. Another version for the last journey is depicted on a larnax from Kavrochori of Heraklion. Here the depiction of a chariot in a 'paradisiacal landscape' shows that, in addition to crossing the waves, the deceased also needed land transport.

The chariot here is empty and the horses are lyring on the ground. The image may refer to a horse sacrifice in honour of the deceased, an act known from actual examples, such as in the

193

tholos tomb at Fourni Archanes and in Mycenaean tombs in the Argolid and at Marathon. The 'spatial planning' of the Minoan paradise is succinctly presented on the larnax from Klima in Mesara. All sides are bordered by marine nautilus-argonauts and wavy framing, images that in the pictorial language of the larnakes signify land in or beyond the sea borders. On one large side, the octopuses in the lower part denote the marine world, while the tree, ibexes and bulls in the upper zone represent the flora and fauna of the land. The meaning is condensed and codified: the place of final destination is a distant land beyond the sea. The other side was decorated with masses of aquatic plants with rivers and a majestic throne with a figure behind it, perhaps the patron god of the dead on his podium giving out his final judgment.

Another theological view of the underworld and its gods is illustrated on a larnax from Knossos. Two female figures are depicted in the panels, of which the first on the left addresses the second on the right through an adoring gesture. The first one may be the deceased, the second one is the goddess with raised hands, a 'holy' gesture seen time and again by the clay female idols. A divine figure with raised hands is also present on the narrow side of a larnax

194. Larnax with a composition of a griffin, lily-papyrus and religious symbols, horns of consecration and double axes. Palaikastro, 1370-1300 BC.

195. Larnax with a dense composition of papyrus flowers. Gazi, 1300-1200 BC.

196. Larnax with a representation of a sailing ship, symbolizing the transition of the deceased to 'islands of the blessed'. Gazi, 1300-1250 BC.

197. Bath-shaped larnax with representation of cows and a suckling calf. Gournia, 1350-1250 BC.

194

from Vatheianos Kampos, confirming the propagation of the representation of the established type of the goddess with raised arms in the funerary sphere. The spread and adoption of symbols from the everyday context, as well as the earlier palatial modes of worship are also shown by the presence of other well-known subjects of Minoan religion, such as the griffin on a larnax from Palaikastro, the horns of consecration, the double axes and the lily-papyrus plants (**Fig. 194**). Together they declare that the otherworldly garden of the blessed dead is sacred and under the protection of divine powers. The bath-shaped larnakes come from workshops in eastern Crete. Octopuses and fish that 'swim' on the inner walls of one such from Pachyammos refer evocatively to the marine world and the journey to otherworldly islands. Papyri and cows, one seen nursing her calf on a larnax from Gournia (**Fig. 197**), compose the image of the idyllic meadow in Paradise filled with life.

CASE 128. THE SETTLEMENTS OF KNOSSOS AND PHAISTOS

The practice of organizing large-scale banquets continues, particularly in the major settlements of the Postpalatial period. Impressive vessels, such as kraters, are used to hold the wine for the decanting vessels. Compositions of well-designed curvilinear patterns and antithetical birds in synchronized 'dancing' movements mark the last flicker of the decorative style that generally dominated Bronze Age Cretan vase painting. Images from real life are captured by some clay figurines, such as the jar-laden pack-animal from Phaistos and the bearded man from Knossos.

195

197

196

ROOM XIII
MINOAN MURALS. The World of the Court and the World of Nature

The creation of wall paintings that carry symbolic themes goes back to the Neolithic period in Anatolia. As a complex visual art, with images and patterns from both formal and everyday life as well as from the natural world, wall painting appears on funerary monuments in Egypt as early as the 3rd millennium BC. The Minoan wall paintings, which certainly drew ideas and inspiration from the older Egyptian ones, constitute the oldest large-scale wall paintings in the Greek area, spanning from the 19th-18th to the 14th centuries BC.

With the technique of fresco painting, the colours are spread on the wet surface of the plaster before it dries, so that their penetration into the core of the plaster is achieved, resulting in durability over time and limited wear. A grid of fine horizontal and vertical incisions helps the artist draw accurately and quickly before the plaster dries. More rarely, in a variation of the concave (*incavo*) technique, the basic design is impressed by a tool or by cutting into the surface of the plaster, and then the resulting groove is filled with thick paint. Moreover, the Minoans also used the technique of relief wall painting: the relief is created by superimposing layers of plaster before painting. In this way, anatomical details are rendered with plasticity and more naturalness and intensity can be achieved. Another category – the miniature fresco, with tiny figures painted with thin brushes – is chosen to render large, crowded gatherings and dense narrative scenes, which would not be fully developed on a larger scale.

The colours used are mostly ochre-producing earths and other natural substances: riebeckite for grey-blue, iron oxides like hematite and limonite for red, yellow and brown, coal carbon and ash for black and grey, and the lime plaster itself for white. Only the 'Egyptian blue' (made of sand, sodium salts, copper and calcium carbonate) is a chemically synthetic and man-made material. Additional hues and tones are created by mixing or diluting the primary colours.

Mural compositions with various figurative and decorative themes, periodically renewed throughout the Neopalatial and Final Palatial periods (1700-1300 BC), covered the walls of palaces, central buildings and town houses, as a means of projecting the glamour and wealth of the leading classes. Such pictorial compositions ultimately vanished after the fall of the palaces, verifying through their disappearance that mural painting was always an art of the palace and urban elite.

Wall-paintings of Minoan style, technique and repertoire appear from the 17th to the 15th centuries BC in settlements with a strong Minoan presence on the islands of the Aegean, such as Thera, Melos, Kea, Rhodes but also Miletus, and even in Egypt and the East. The art of wall painting also passed to Mycenaean mainland Greece, where it flourished in the palatial environment until the end of the Mycenaean world, in the 13th century BC.

Based on the pictorial content of the Minoan murals, two major thematic groups can be distinguished. One, 'The World of the Court', includes images of life and ritual in palaces, large city buildings and mansions. The second, 'The World of Nature', is made up of subjects and compositions from the natural environment, namely animals and plants of land, sea and air.

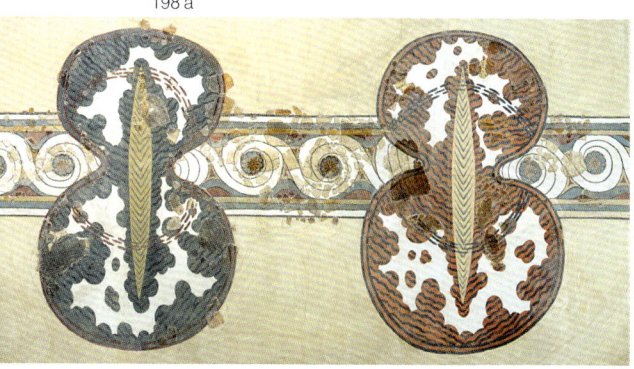

CASES 129-141. THE WORLD OF THE COURT

This broad thematic unit is made up of the large images of palatial events, festive days, but also includes examples of the strong secular and religious symbols of authority and power employed by the ruler and the ruling class.

CASE 129. PAINTED FIGURE-OF-EIGHT SHIELDS

Large-scale representations set in a row adorned the walls of the flanking colonnades of the Grand Staircase at Knossos during the Mycenaean Final Palatial period (1450-1350/1300 BC). They copy real shields made of spotted ox hide stretched over a wooden or metal frame that would have been hung on the walls (Fig. 198). The figure-of-eight shield, a symbol known from many depictions, conveyed a clear message of protection as well as of deterrence, in the context of a 'military' iconography bolstering the power of the leader.

CASES 130, 131. THE PROCESSION FRESCO. THE RHYTON-BEARER

A magnificent composition of hundreds of figures in a dense arrangement and near life-size covered the walls of the Procession Corridor that runs from the western courtyard of the

198a, b. The fresco of the "Figure-of-Eight Shields" from Knossos (1450-1350/1300 BC) and their painted reconstruction in the Hall of the Double Axes / King's Hall (by Piet de Jong

199. The "Rhyton-Bearer" depiction of a youth, carrying a rhyton – made of silver as indicated by its blue colour. It is part of the "Procession Fresco", a composition of many figures, who bear gifts to the anax/lord. Knossos, 1500-1400 BC.

palace of Knossos to the Great Propylaea leading up to the official apartments on the first-floor on the western wing. It represents an actual ritual procession of gift-bearers to the *wanax* (leading male person in the Mycenaean hierarchy): they march in line, as did the Minoans in Egyptian frescoes seen in the tombs of dignitaries such as Rekhmire (image in Room V). The aim is, as in Egypt, to display the wealth, power and prestige of the recipient of the offerings. The participants also belong to the upper class, as is evidenced by their ornate loincloths with their woven motifs, dexterously designed with the help of an incised fine grid. The 'Rhyton-bearer' (Fig. 199), at an almost life-size scale, is the best preserved in the procession. A young man with a richly decorated body and loincloth is depicted carrying a large rhyton, the blue colour

200. The 'Tripartite Shrine', a miniature fresco depicting a crowd gathering in front of a shrine. Knossos, 1600-1450 BC.

201. Fragment from the fresco of the 'Tripartite Shrine', with a neatly-drawn depiction of a group of women conversing. Knossos, 1600-1450 BC.

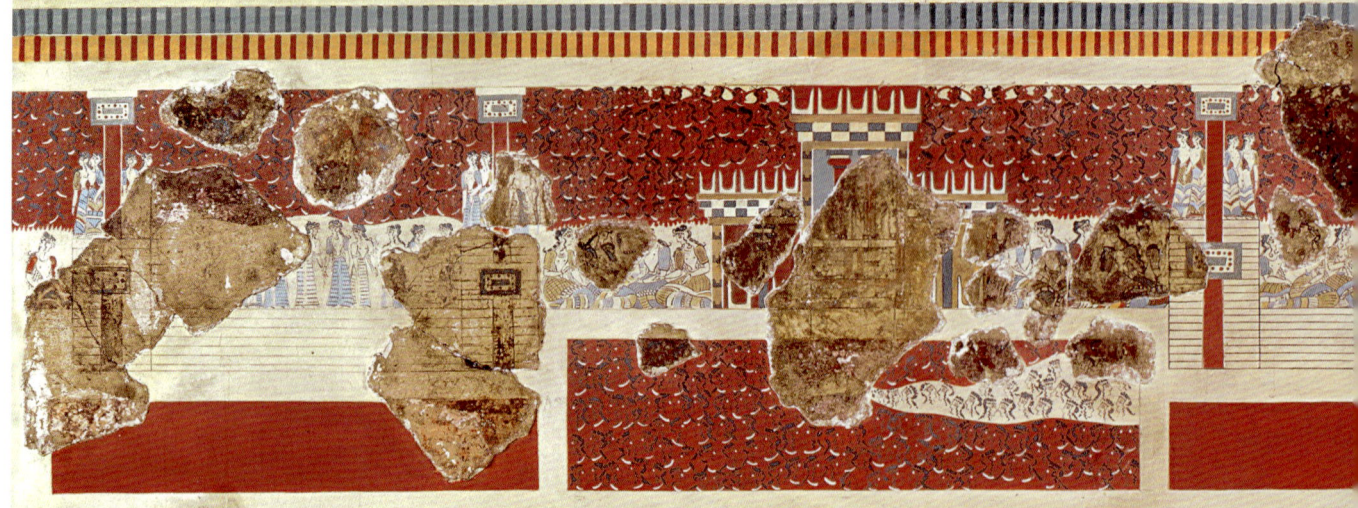

of which suggests that it was made of silver. It seems that ritual scenes were also interspersed throughout the procession, as indicated by the elongated fragment from the lower part of the fresco that preserves the legs of two groups of male figures advancing in opposite directions, converging towards a priestess (Room VIII, 92). The fresco is dated to 1500-1400 BC.

CASE 132. MINIATURE WALL PAINTINGS. THE TRIPARTITE SHRINE. THE SACRED GROVE

Many wall-painting fragments from Knossos depict small-scale crowds in front of building façades bedecked with colonnades or balconies. They are thought to capture moments from great festive days in the palace.

In the fresco of the *Tripartite Shrine* or *Grandstand Fresco* (1600-1450 BC) (**Fig. 200**) the crowds are gathered in a rectangular space in front of a tripartite shrine with columns; it is constructed on a rectangular base with a frieze of semi-rosettes and is flanked by stepped platforms supporting colonnades. On these stand or sit female figures who appear to be conversing animatedly (**Fig. 201**). The assembled crowd is depicted conventionally, with only the outlines of the heads drawn on a surface which is painted dark red for the men and left white for the women. The whole composition conveys an atmosphere of the hubbub of a gathering inside and outside the palace and its central courtyard (the rectangle in front of the sanctuary), or some other stadium-like space within the city, equipped with platforms and a sanctuary façade.

Another crowded assembly is depicted in the *Sacred Grove* wall-painting from Knossos (1600-1450 BC), showing crowds of men and women among trees and a courtyard crossed by paved walkways. Perhaps it is the western courtyard of the palace, which has such raised pathways. Other fresco fragments from Knossos depict façades and balconies of buildings with parapets. Other representations include scenes of procession rituals with a priest in a chariot, a palanquin with a seated figure carried by servants, and a bull-leaping scene with a female figure.

All these creations date to 1450-1350/1300 BC. In another fragment, the theme of the Minoan labyrinth is represented in a linear design. It is dated to 1650-1500 BC. Despite the gulf of time, the pattern is strikingly reminiscent of the labyrinth representations on classical coins from Knossos. Interesting fragments of miniature frescoes from Tylissos, dating from 1650-1450 BC, depict the transportation of amphorae, a procession of boxers and groups of women.

CASES 133, 134. PROCESSIONS OF PRIESTS AND DANCES FROM AGIA TRIADA

Three fresco compositions date to the final palace period, 1450-1350/1300 BC. The first depicts a procession with a priestess at the front and behind her two goats or deer. The altar on the left indicates their impending sacrifice. The second piece shows groups of women dancing and the third a procession of priests carrying buckets accompanied by a lyre-player, recalling similar scenes from the Agia Triada sarcophagus.

CASE 135. THE GODDESSES OR PRIESTESSES OF PSEIRA

Two incomplete relief frescoes from the islet of Pseira (1450 BC) depict two female priestly figures or deities seated on rocks. The subtle and rich decoration of the garment, which was painted with a finely incised grid as a guide, and the realistic three-dimensional shaping of their chests and shoulders is impressive.

CASE 136. THE PROGRAM OF THE FRESCOS OF THE THRONE ROOM

The gypsum throne of Knossos was flanked by wingless griffins painted on the walls. They act as its sturdy and vigilant guards (**Fig. 202**). From this fragmentary composition comes the impressive griffin with a crest on its head and polychrome spirals together with papyrus flowers on its neck; it lies recumbent on the ground with beak raised, among reedy plants. In addition to the griffin, images to the right of the throne also belong to the same composition. Here occurs the 'sacred' pattern of the biconcave altar right next to the throne, a flowering palm tree that appears to grow from the throne, and another griffin of which only a leg has been preserved. A second palm tree would have been symmetrically placed on the other side of the throne. The frescoes date to 1450–1350/1300 BC, meaning the first period of the palace's operation.

CASE 137. THE 'PRINCE OF THE LILIES' OR 'PRIEST-KING'

The famous relief fresco of the 'Prince of the Lilies' (**Fig. 203**) is an iconic and well-known image of the Minoan world. It was discovered at the southern entrance of the palace of Knossos and belonged to a procession scene moving towards the central courtyard. The shape of the lithe young man was reconstructed from three large sections and some smaller ones; it has received many modern additions and reinterpretations. He wears the typical Minoan loincloth, as well as a necklace with beads in the shape of papyrus-lily heads and on his head an impressive crown decorated with papyrus-lily flowers and

202

peacock feathers. According to Evans, it depicts the 'Priest-King' of Knossos. However, based on newer restorations, the fragments are thought to belong to a boxer or a god, while the crown belongs to another being altogether, perhaps a sphinx or a goddess. It is dated to 1600-1450 BC.

CASE 138. 'THE GRIFFINS'

Tethered to columns, the relief griffins symbolize the palace's permanent guards. This relief fresco with its white griffins on a blue background adorned a large hall next to the Great Staircase of Knossos, along with religious symbols and other relief frescoes depicting sports (Room VI, 61). It is dated to 1600-1450 BC.

CASE 139. 'THE BULL'

A symbol of power and enforcement, in keeping with the characteristics that any powerful dynasty should possess, is the bull of Knossos. It was the subject of many wall-painting compositions with an emphasis on the palatial sport of bull-leaping. The relief bust of the 'Bull' (**Fig. 204**) comes from the 'West Bastion' portico at the northern entrance of the palace of Knossos and dates to 1600-1450 BC. It belonged to a wider composition depicting a bull hunt in a rocky landscape with olive trees. It is a premium creation of Minoan naturalism, of special artistic quality and expressive power. The anatomical features and modelled structure of the

202. The 'Throne Room' of Knossos (1450-1350/1300 BC) with the throne flanked by a fresco composition with wingless griffins and palm trees. (digital representation by Y. Galanakis, E. Tsitsa, U. Günkel-Maschek).

203. Relief fresco of the 'Prince of the Lilies', a well-known image of a young man with an impressive crown of lily-papyrus and peacock feathers, according to the restoration of the figure by A. Evans. Knossos, 1600-1450 BC.

204. Relief fresco with a life-size bust of a bull, a naturalistic work of unique quality. It is part of a figurative composition of bull hunting in a rocky landscape with olive trees. Knossos, west bastion of the North Entrance, 1600-1450 BC

head in side view are realistically and accurately rendered. The dramatic tone of the animal's exertions to escape its pursuers, or to confront them, is captured with unique expressive power in the bulging eyes, the outstretched ears, open mouth and nostrils dilated from its hard breathing. In no other Minoan work of art was the intensity of the moment and the physical surge of the tempestuous movement of the attacking animal so convincingly expressed.

CASE 140. 'THE LADIES IN BLUE'

The fragmentarily preserved fresco with the 'Ladies in Blue' (**Fig. 205**) gives us a taste of the coquetry of the Ladies of the Court. The women are set on a blue background, with richly decorated clothes, rows of jewellery at the neck and arms and in their hair. They form an eloquent image of the affluence, sophistication and stylishness of the women who lived in the palace environment. This work comes from the palace at Knossos and dates to 1600-1450 BC.

CASE 141. 'THE CAMPSTOOL FRESCO'.
'LA PARISIENNE'

Palace banquets were always splendid opportunities for displaying the abundance of goods and a refined behaviour that defined the elite. Such an image is offered by the so-called 'Campstool Fresco' from Knossos of 1450-1350/1300 BC. Pairs of communicants are seated on folding seats and raise 'communion cups' and goblets, in a toast.

205. The 'Ladies in Blue', a fragmentarily preserved fresco, depicting women of the palatial court, with rich clothes and jewellery. Knossos, 1600-1450 BC.

206. The famous 'La Parisienne', fragment from the 'Campstool Fresco', depicting a young woman with strong features and makeup, probably a priestess as indicated by the 'sacred knot' on her back. Knossos, 1350-1300 BC.

207. The 'Dolphin Fresco', probably a floor composition, depicts dolphins swimming against a background that indicates the iridescence of the sea. Knossos, 1600-1450 BC.

206

The stylish 'La Parisienne' (**Fig. 206**), as Evans called her, belongs to the same composition. She was depicted on a larger scale and could therefore be a prominent figure in the symposium. She is a young woman with strong Mediterranean features and red-painted lips. She appears to have been a priestess, as indicated by the 'sacral knot' symbol attached to the hem of the garment at her back.

CASES 142-149. THE WORLD OF NATURE: LANDSCAPES, SEASCAPES AND MINOAN GARDENS
The Minoans were particularly fond of depicting life scenes within the natural landscape of Crete and in the water of the sea. They did not faithfully copy their models from nature, but added their own contributions, sometimes exceeding the boundaries of realism.

CASE 142. THE DOLPHIN FRESCO from the Queen's Hall in the palace of Knossos draws its patterns from the sea world (**Fig. 207**). Two dolphins swim among small fish against the background of the iridescent net created by play of the sun on the seabed. The composition arguably adorned a floor. It is dated to 1600-1450 BC.

207

208

CASE 143. THE PARTRIDGE FRESCO

This fresco depicts the most characteristic bird of the Cretan wildlife (Fig. 208). On the top zone of the walls of an open pavilion in the building complex of the 'Caravan-Serai' at Knossos, partridges are painted with fine brushwork and in a variety of colours. They are illustrated among rocks, polychrome pebbles, reeds and bushes. The white and black backgrounds in different parts of the composition probably indicate that the scenes unfold during the day and night respectively. The work is dated to 1600-1450 BC.

FRAGMENTS OF WALL PAINTINGS

Fragments of figurative landscape compositions, the oldest known to date, come from the palace and settlement of Galatas in Heraklion and they date from 1700-1650 BC. A framed structure enclosing a plant, rocks and bushy plants are depicted. Parts of the paintings from the House of Frescoes depict various plants, a waterfall and the 'portrait' of a monkey. They are dated to 1600-1500 BC.

208. The 'Partridge Fresco', a polychrome composition, depicts partridges in a rocky, verdant natural landscape. Knossos, 1600-1450 BC.

209. The 'Garland Fresco' depicts a row of wreaths, composed of various flowers and plants. Knossos, 1600-1450 BC.

209

THE GARLANDS FRESCO

In a wall painting from Knossos, a series of wreaths made of anemones, roses, oregano or ivy, red lilies, crocuses, and myrtle or olive leaves are depicted (Fig. 209). In addition to their decorative value, they seem to have also had a religious significance, since they symbolize the efflorescence and regeneration of nature over time, a central theme in Minoan religion. It is dated to 1600-1450 BC.

CASES 145-146. THE HOUSE OF FRESCOS. THE BLUE BIRD

These two showcases display two large pieces from this composition (Fig. 210) which once adorned a spacious room of a house near the palace of Knossos. Cretan plants grow among the rocks – crocuses, irises, papyrus, ivy, myrtles, wild pomegranates and reeds. Monkeys run about between them, while a blue bird is depicted sitting on a rock. The composition is crossed by streams, one even with a waterfall (a pictorial restoration is given in showcase 144). The plants grow in the rough ground as well as in the rocky upper level of the composition, thus creating the illusion of a multi-dimensional and a bilaterally inverted space.

210. The 'Blue Bird', in a wall-fresco composition with monkeys, is depicted sitting on rocks, among various plants of the Cretan flora and streams. Knossos, 1600-1500 BC.

CASES 147-148. THE LILY FRESCO

The program of wall-paintings in the Villa of the Lilies at Amnisos, with its impressive plants and flowers, transports us to the environment of urban and sub-urban mansions. In the stylized composition (**Fig. 212**), stems of white lilies and red irises are shown growing in flower beds or pots, giving the impression of an organized and fenced town garden. It is a direct testimony to the high standard of living, the love of flowers and the pursuit of beauty and perfection by the wealthy townspeople. The composition used a combination of the fresco and the *incavo* techniques: it is dated to 1600-1500 BC.

CASE 149. FLOOR SEASCAPE

A seascape composition covered the floor of the sanctuary in Agia Triada. It is a dense composition of dolphins, fish and an octopus swimming among rocks at the bottom of the sea (Fig. 211). Thus, whoever entered the sanctuary would have the impression that he is literally walking on the sea – and that he has become a denizen of the underwater world and its living beings. It is dated to 1350-1300 BC.

DECORATIVE THEMES ON FLOOR FROM PHAISTOS

The oldest known example of painting employing decorative patterns on plaster is exhibited in the same showcase. Identical four-lobed shapes were created by the *incavo* technique, by repeatedly pressing a tool into the fresh mortar: the shallow cavities created were then filled with thick reddish paint. It comes from a floor of a room of the Protopalatial period of the palace of Phaistos and dates to 1800-1700 BC.

211. Seascape floor fresco composition with dolphins, fish and a red octopus, whose swimming is reminiscent of dancing. Agia Triada, 1350-1300 BC.

212. The 'Lilies Fresco', with stylized plants of white lilies and red iris, evokes the image of a walled garden with flower beds. Amnisos, 1600-1500 BC.

ROOM XIV
MINOAN LEGACY

MINOAN LEGACY. CRETAN MYTHS TO LATE ANTIQUITY

Information panels, pictorial material and digital-interactive aids present the mythical as well as the real material impact of the Minoan civilization both in its wider modern cultural environment as well as in later ancient Greek and Roman art.

THE MYTHS

The nexus of the beguiling Cretan myths that drew upon themes and figures from the glorious Minoan past is an important component in the body of ancient Greek mythology. Their imaginative narratives are centred, directly or indirectly, around the legendary Minos, king of Knossos and Crete. According to legend, his father was Zeus, the supreme god. His mother was Europa – 'she of the broad gaze', as her name means – a princess of Phoenicia. Zeus transformed into a bull **(Fig. 213)**, he abducted her and brought her to Crete. From their union, three sons were born: Minos, the iconic leader of Crete, the wise and just Rhadamanthys, a judge of the afterlife in Hades with Minos, and Sarpedon, who became king in Lycia in Asia Minor. Minos married the daughter of Helios, Pasiphae, which means 'the bright one'. Pasiphae lusted after the sacred bull that Poseidon had given to Minos: to attract its attention she hid inside a statue of a cow made by the ingenious craftsman Daedalus. From this sinful union was born the Minotaur, an anthropomorphic monster with the body of a man and the head of a bull, which Minos imprisoned in the complex Labyrinth, also the work of Daedalus. Seven young men and seven young women sent by Athens as a blood tribute to Minos were thrown in the Labyrinth to become Minotaur's prey every year. Theseus, prince of Athens, killed the Minotaur and with the help of Ariadne, daughter of Minos, managed to get out of the Labyrinth by following the unravelled ball of thread he left behind him. Theseus took Ariadne with him when leaving Crete, but abandoned her in Naxos, where she was seen and taken as wife by the god Dionysus **(Fig. 214)**.

The famous craftsman Daedalus created wonderful works for Minos, who kept him captive in Crete. He escaped with his son, Icarus, by flight, with the help of wax and feather wings he made for the two of them. But Icarus disobeying his father's advice flew too high; the sun melted the wax in his wings and so he fell into the sea and drowned.

According to myth, the guardian of Crete was the bronze winged giant Talos, who ran daily from one end of the island to the other, carrying tablets with the laws written on them. He drove away any enemy ships in the sea by throwing huge stones at them.

Other stories refer to the colonization of the Aegean islands by the sons and grandsons of Minos, to the intermarriages, to the military exploits and adventures of his descendants, but also to the murder of Minos himself in Ka-

213

mikos, Sicily, where he had arrived in pursuit of Daedalus. According to legend, the mighty king of Crete was murdered by the daughters of the local king Kokalos by having boiling water poured onto him while taking a bath.

Aspects of the main Minoan myths – the abduction of Europa, the slaying of the Minotaur, the meeting of Ariadne with Dionysus, Daedalus and Icarus – were depicted in works of ancient art, especially those from the Hellenistic to the late Roman periods. The memory of Crete's glorious Minoan past was also preserved in the works of ancient Greek and Latin literature. Chroniclers, poets, dramatists, comedians, geographers, travellers, historians throughout antiquity referenced the mythical tradition, highlighting the power, prosperity and cultural reach of Minoan Crete. Homer mentions Minos conversing with Zeus and King Idomeneus, grandson of Minos, as a brave warrior in the Trojan War. Hesiod considers Minos as the foremost among kings. Plato in his *Laws* singles out and praises the legal system of Crete and Aristotle in the *Politics* does the same for the administrative-state organization. Ancient authors such as Antiphanes, Sophocles, Euripides and Aristophanes wrote works inspired by Cretan myths, most of which have not survived. Historians like Thucydides and Herodotus refer to Minos's rule in the Aegean, to the Minoan colonization of the islands and the Minoan rule of the sea.

214

MYTH AND REALITY. THE MINOAN THALOSSACRACY

Archaeological research from the beginning of the last century to the present day has verified that some of the vivid Cretan myths contain kernels of truth from Minoan times. The figure of Minos remains of course in the realm of myth and cannot be determined by historical evidence, unlike, for example, the pharaohs of Egypt. However, the labyrinthine palace uncovered at Knossos is indeed the most imposing monument of Minoan Crete, a centre of organized administration, as the preserved records show, and ostentatious luxury, manifested in its construction, decoration and furnishing. Some earlier researchers have identified it with the mythical Labyrinth, and perhaps it is no coincidence that a Linear B tablet was found there that mentions a 'potnia of the Labyrinth' (See Room IX/Fig. 149). Another tablet records an offering of oil to the Daedaleion sanctuary, echoing the name of the legendary craftsman Daedalus. The bull, co-protagonist in key myths, is a well-known emblematic pattern in Minoan iconography, especially when connected to Knossos. The Minotaur seems to indeed refer to Minoan myth, since a bull-man figure is depicted on a Minoan sard seal and on a sealing. The two circular masonry platforms or dancing-floors that were uncovered not far from the palace have been associated with Ariadne's dancing grounds, as described by Homer: in his account, the young men and women danced in a circle on the dancing floor at Knossos, led by the princess Ariadne and accompanied by music and demonstrations by two acrobats. A pair of acrobats engaged in synchronized tumbling

213. Europa and the Zeus-as-Bull on an Attic krater of 480 BC, a work of the 'Berlin painter'.
© Archaeological Museum of Tarquinia, Italy.

214. The wedding of Dionysus and Ariadne. Detail of a relief representation on the bronze krater of Derveni, 330-320 BC. © Archaeological Museum of Thessaloniki, Greece.

215. Drawing reconstruction of a wall painting with bull-leaping against a labyrinth background, from Avaris, Egypt, 1500-1450 BC. (Archive of Prof. M. Bietak).

216. Minoan envoy carrying a vessel in the form of a bull's head. Fresco in the Egyptian tomb of Rekhmire. 1500-1400 BC (Photo archive of the New York Metropolitan Museum of Art).

are depicted in exactly this way both on a Minoan seal and on a painted portable altar.

Archaeological investigations continuously reveal evidence of the Minoan reach throughout the Aegean and the Peloponnese to the coasts of Asia Minor, the shores of the eastern Mediterranean and in areas of Egypt. Thus they confirm the core of historical truth contained in the ancient reports, such as Thucydides', about Minoan rule over the sea and the islands. Coastal cities-colonies are recognized as port trading-stations: they display Minoan characteristics in all kinds of artwork in iconography and style, but also demonstrate influences on architecture, writing and metric systems. Thereby was created a dense network of both commercial-economic and ideological-cultural penetration. In the Cyclades, there is Thera with its amazing Minoan frescoes, but also Kea, Melos and Naxos. In the Dodecanese, the islands of Rhodes, Kos, Samos, Kalymnos, Kasos and Karpathos are influenced, as are those of Samothraki and Lemnos in the northern Aegean. Minoan finds of exceptional quality have been discovered in the western Cretan Sea, Kythera and in the Peloponnese, Mycenae, Pylos, Vapheio, as well as in Aegina. Further off, on the coast of Asia Minor, the important site of Miletus displays a strong Minoan presence as does the area around Smyrna. On the Syro-Palestinian coast and in the interior of Syria and Lebanon, Minoan items, presence and know-how touched Ugarit, Byblos and Qatna, in Israel El Kabri and in Turkey Alalakh. The Minoan finds on these sites enhance the information acquired from the archives of the palaces of the prehistoric kingdoms of the East: at Mari in Syria near the Euphrates there is a record of an ornamental sword and a metal vase of Cretan manufacture. A poetic text from Ugarit of the 14th century BC contains an invocation to the goddess to call from Crete (Kaphtor) the god of art to adorn the king's palace. Another record mentions a Cretan agent in Ugarit who was supplied with tin from Mari. Even more emphatically, the wall paintings in Egyptian tombs of the 15th century BC depict Minoans, the Keftiu as they are called in the Egyptian language, carrying precious Minoan artefacts to the pharaoh (**Fig. 216**). Frescoes of Minoan technique and subject matter, such as the bull-leaping scenes from the palace at Avaris/Tel el Daba (**Fig. 215**) in the Nile delta, are significant testimonies to the power and appeal of the Minoan world.

CASE 150. Black-figure lekythos depicting the slaying of the Minotaur by Theseus; early 5th century BC (Donation of the National Archaeological Museum of Athens).

ROOM XXV
MINOAN ECHOES
Cretan Myths from the Renaissance to the Modern Era

With an introductory text, further enabled by images with subtitles and an interactive video screen, the breadth of the appeal and symbolism of ancient Cretan myths in modern times is highlighted.

Already in the Middle Ages, and especially from the Renaissance onwards, many Cretan myths were included in the artistic repertoire, as a consequence of the general interest in classical antiquity and the Greco-Roman heritage, of which Cretan mythology is a part. The well-known myths of the abduction of Europa by Zeus in the guise of a bull, of Ariadne by Theseus and her abandonment in Naxos, of the Minotaur and the Labyrinth, of Daedalus and Icarus lended fertile ground for artistic reworkings according to the stylistic trends of each era and the pictorial choices of their creators.

From the 14th century onwards, Cretan myths are depicted in paintings and drawings, in sculptures and reliefs, engravings and etchings, tapestries and illustrated manuscripts. Leading artists – from Giotto, Titian **(Fig. 217)**, Veronese to Rubens, Van Dyck, Sokoloff, Canova, Daumier and Gauguin – all signed works inspired by 'Minoan' mythology. Michelangelo in the 16th century depicted in the Sistine Chapel Minos in the Underworld **(Fig. 218)**, Heindel composed the opera *Ariadne in Crete* in 1734 and Mozart the opera *Idomeneus King of Crete* in 1781.

The quest for innovation in European art and intellectual circles from the end of the 19th cen-

217. 'Abduction of Europa', V. Titian (1559-1562). © I. St. Gardner Museum, Boston.
218. 'Minos in the Underworld', Michelangelo, The Final Judgment (detail). Sistine Chapel (1536-1541), **Vatican.**

tury and the first decades of the 20th coincided with the sensational unveiling of the palace of Knossos by Arthur Evans. Mythical tradition now corresponded to material reality. Moreover, Minoan culture seemed to possess and anticipate elements of modern European culture: organized trade and expansion along sea routes, rule of law, love of nature, social participation of women and, moreover, the earliest use of writing in the geographical space of modern-day Europe. Europe indeed owes its very name to the woman at the heart of the archetypal Cretan myth, the mother of Minos. Thus, the eminent Gordon Childe characterized the brilliant prehistoric civilization of Crete as the 'first European civilization', while thinkers such as J. Myers, A. Toynbee, O. Spangler and also S. Freud included references to this culture in their work. At the same time, artists recognized in Minoan pictorial art, with its inherent tendencies towards post-realism and abstraction, the features of modernism, especially Art Nouveau, thus giv-

ing new impetus to borrowing themes from the Cretan mythological cycle. Some works of the time are the 'Sleeping Ariadne' series by J. De Chirico, but also the appearance of the Minotaur in sculptures by O. Rodin or even the opera *Ariadne in Naxos* by R. Strauss in 1912.

Special emphasis on the Cretan mythical repertoire was given during the interwar period at the hands of the modernist artists, especially the Paris surrealist circle, who were inspired by the well-known Cretan myths. First and foremost, Picasso used the Minotaur as the main subject in a series of works; he used him to illustrate the first issue of the art review *Minotaure* (**Fig. 219**), published in the 1930s in Paris by Stratis Eleftheriadis-Teriade. The covers of subsequent issues – always depicting the Minotaur – were executed by a series of great artists, including A. Derain (**Fig. 220**), M. Duchamp, H. Miró, S. Dali, A. Matisse, R. Magritte (**Fig. 221**), A Masson, D. Rivera and M. Ernst (**Fig. 222**). After the war, the surrealist N. Eggonopoulos painted in a series of works the murder of the Minotaur (**Fig. 223**) and completed his Cretan mythological theme with the 'Rape of Europe' and 'Daedalos'. The myth of the flight and fall of young Icarus, which can symbolize man's futile desire to break the bonds of gravity and fly free above and beyond the earth, is a theme that maintained a strong symbolism throughout the ages. The subject was addressed by important poets and writers such as S. Baudelaire and G. Apollinaire, in whose work Icarus forms a pattern with multiple-layered symbolic readings. Other painters also took up the subject: from P. Bruegel the Elder (1560) and P. Rubens (1636) (**Fig. 225**), to M. Chagall (1975) and finally Picasso, who created (1958) panels with the 'Fall of Icarus' that adorn the main UNESCO building.

A. Matisse in 1941 depicts Icarus with a red bullet in his heart between flashes of explosions (**Fig. 224**), a clear semantic symbolism for freedom in the midst of the Nazi occupation of Europe.

Patterns of Cretan mythology are recognized, although transfigured, in the works of well-known writers, such as A. Gide, J. Joyce, H.L. Borges, A. Sikelianos and N. Kazantzakis.

The seductive Cretan myths continue their journey through time, imperishable and untarnished to this day, by way of artistic creations of all sorts, be they grand-scale works of broad conception or small glimpses of details within the mythological fabric.

219-222. Covers of the art magazine Minotaure (Minotaur) by P. Picasso (1933), A. Derain (1933), R. Magritte (1937), M. Ernst (1938). The magazine was published in Paris by Stratis Eleftheriadis-Teriade.

223. 'Theseus kills the Minotaur', N. Eggonopoulos (1961).

224. 'Ikaros', A. Matisse (1943-1944), from the publication 'Jazz' (1947) by Stratis Eleftheriadis-Teriade. © Museum of Modern Art, New York.

225. 'The Fall of Icarus', P. Rubens (1636), © Royal Museum of Fine Arts, Brussels.

ROOM XV
CRETE FROM THE EARLY IRON AGE TO LATE ANTIQUITY
A. Geometric, Archaic and Classical Period. 11th–4th centuries BC.

CITIES AND SANCTUARIES

CITIES. THE INSTITUTIONAL BASIS OF THE 'CRETAN POLITY'

After the fall of the Mycenaean centres, during the first centuries of Dorian rule from the 11th century BC onwards, life continues at the broadly established sites such as Knossos, while new settlements are created in mountainous locations, in Karfi, Kavousi, Vrokastro and elsewhere. During the following periods, settlements gradually multiply as a result of rapid economic and population growth. From the end of the 8th century BC several are transformed into *Poleis*; that is, autonomous political entities with a state structure that control a specific territory, enact laws, make alliances or wage wars; from the 5th century BC they issue coins. Amongst these emergent cities were Gortyna, Knossos, Phaistos, Lyttos, Arkades and Eltyna in central Crete, Praisos, Dreros, Lato in the east, with Kydonia, Aptera, Axos and Eleftherna in the west.

The 'Cretan Polity' mentioned by Plato is organized on a tribal basis. Each Polity is controlled by the '*kosmoi*', who exercise political and military power and are elected for a specific term. Another important political institution is the *Gerousia*, a council of elders with supervisory capacities. The corps of *Ippeis*, the cavalry, made up from men of aristocratic families performs official duties. The *Ecclesia* or Assembly, consisting of the male citizens, decides by acclaim all important matters of the City in the *Agora*, the centre of all public activities. The basic institutional unit is the *Andreion*, which oversees the concerns and matters of each tribe as well as the education system for young people until adulthood. The *Andreion* was housed in a public building that housed the city's never extinguished 'common hearth' and men's dining facilities. Temples and sanctuaries are part of the urban fabric; they were placed in the outskirts of the cities, as were the *gymnasia* for the training of young people.

Religious life is intertwined with social and political structures. Terms of civil and criminal law and treaties between cities are recorded on stone inscriptions set up in public places and temples. Temples and sanctuaries received a multitude of votive offerings from the faithful and they were decorated with sculptures commissioned and paid for by both the public purse and private donors. They function as focal points of large-scale gatherings of the local population and centres of social cohesion.

WALL TO THE RIGHT OF THE ENTRANCE.
INSCRIPTIONS

Two inscriptions of the 4th century BC written in the unknown '*Eteocretan*' language, come from Praisos in eastern Crete. The words are written in the Greek alphabet but are not Greek. Some scholars believe them to represent the ancient unknown language of the Minoans. Such inscriptions, dating from the 6th to the 2nd centuries BC, have been found in Praisos and Dreros where lived the Eteocretans: they were ancient populations, perhaps with Minoan roots.

Three inscriptions of the 2nd-1st centuries BC from the sanctuary of Zeus Thenatas in Amnisos are dedicated by the '*kosmoi*' of the city, referred to individually by their names.

SETTLEMENTS – DAILY LIFE

The settlements of the period consist of small houses with rudimentary facilities and furnishings that serve daily needs. The larger cities have a developed urban organization and some, such as Gortyna, even dispose fortified citadels. Houses made of rough stone walls, usually single-roomed or with small rooms, are sufficient for a frugal lifestyle. Accordingly, the everyday objects employed are also simple, without any noteworthy decoration. However, the residential installations of this period have not been subject to extensive and systematic research.

CASE 152. THE HOUSE-MODEL FROM TEKE

The image of the simple, but functional one-room house is given by a clay model (**Fig. 226**) from Teke, Knossos dating to the 9th century BC. The door is single-leaf one with a transom and the small windows are set in the side walls. A low parapet running around the flat roof served to collect and drain the rain-water. The furnishings inside are elementary: a bench around the perimeter for the occupants to rest on and a shelf at the back for the placement of household items. The chimney in the centre of the roof indicates the existence of a hearth for cooking and heating.

CASES 151, 153, 154. RESIDENTIAL REMAINS

Utensils and other objects retrieved in the houses of settlements such as Knossos, Vrokastro, Phaistos, Smari and Krousonas are the material remains left by domestic activities. These items include vessels for cooking, transporting food, drinking water and wine, stone tools for grinding and processing agricultural produce, loom weights and spindle-whorls for weaving and spinning wool, bronze needles for sewing clothes, and lamps for light after dark. A tortoise shell, marine shell fossils, small clay balls and pellets may have had a magical-apotropaic use, or in the case of the pellets they might be game pieces.

Local workshops produced clay plaques moulds depicting religious representations, such as the '*Potnios Theron*', master of wild animals, and sphinxes, while finds from small domestic sanctuaries indicate a focus on a simple style of worship of the female deity. Two flutes from Axos and a bronze figurine of a musician, a lyre player, (**Fig. 227**) testify to the use of the same musical instruments depicted on the Agia Triada sarcophagus (Room XII). An image from life in the

226. Model of a one-roomed house. Teke Knossos, 9th c. BC.

227. Bronze figurine of a musician playing the lyre, 8th-7th c. BC.

228

fields is represented by the bronze figure of an ox with a man walking behind him, who carries a knapsack, perhaps with some food for his snack. The spread of heroic myths in Crete is indicated by a fragment of a 7th century pithos from Krousonas (**Fig. 228**) The scene of the murder of a woman by two men is depicted in low relief (**Fig. 228**), while a second female figure is standing next to them. The image seems to derive from the myth of the Atreides: the murder of Clytemnestra by Orestes and Pylades in the presence of Electra, an act of revenge for the murder of Agamemnon by Clytemnestra and Aegisthus. The tragic myth was the subject of Aeschylus' *Oresteia*.

PEDESTAL. STORAGE PITHOI

Many impressive and super-sized pithoi with various relief decorations, coming from Afrati (Arkades), Lyttos and Phaistos, document the activity of specialized ceramic workshops in central Crete. The vases are decorated with repetitive relief geometric and decorative themes made using a matrix: fantasy beings, sphinxes and griffins (**Fig. 229**) and other familiar themes from a life lived close to nature, such as the bull and the rooster. As in the Minoan period, in addition to being utilitarian items for storing goods, the ornate pithoi were possessions that projected the prestige and wealth of their owners. They date to the Archaic period (7th–6th centuries BC), but some were used for centuries, as denotes their discovery in Hellenistic houses (3rd–2nd centuries BC).

228. Fragment of a pithos with a relief scene of the killing of a woman, probably the murder of Clytemnestra, a subject from the Atreides myth. Krousonas, 7th c. BC.

229. Oversized pithoi with decorative subjects and relief griffins. Afrati (Arkades) 6th, 7th c. BC.

230. Bronze shield with relief decoration. Palaikastro, end of 8th c. BC.

229

CASES 155, 156. URBAN SANCTUARIES OF EASTERN CRETE

The finds from sanctuaries large and small, within and beyond the boundaries of settlements and cities, provide evidence both for the religious beliefs and practices and for the social structure of the early Greek communities from the 8th to the 6th centuries BC. The sanctuary of Vrokastro, a mountain settlement in the area of Ierapetra, contained clay figurines of horses, a chariot and clay openwork 'baskets', that are a type of fruit bowl.

From the first millennium BC onwards, during the first centuries of the Dorians's settlement in Crete, Praisos and Dreros are two important cities that yielded particularly interesting findings. They belong to the broader mountainous area occupied by the Eteocretans and it is believed that part of the pre-Dorian population had fled in that location.

Praisos is believed to have been the capital of the Eteocretans, a pre-Hellenic tribe of Crete according to Homer. A strong and autonomous city, especially from the 4th century BC, Praisos was involved in hostilities with neighbouring cities over the sovereignty of the sanctuary of Diktaean Zeus in Palaikastro. This conflict ended in the defeat and destruction of Praisos at the hands of the Hierapytnians in 146 BC.

In a large shrine depository at Praisos dating to the Geometric and Archaic years, figurines were found belonging to a female deity and a fragment, perhaps from a finial of a temple roof, representing a female figure with a snake, reminiscent of the Minoan snake goddess. Other finds of interest are a male figurine of the kouros type and a large seated lion figurine of clay. Offerings left in the sanctuary by hoplite warriors are models of bronze weapons, shields, cuirasses, helmets and *mitres*, a metal plate protecting the abdomen.

From Dreros, another important city in eastern Crete, comes the bronze monstrosity of a *Gorgon* of apotropaic purpose and a metal plate in the form of Athena *Promachos* (leading in the fight). In the temple of Delphic Apollo in the Agora of Dreros, inscribed stone slabs with legal texts from the 7th century BC, the oldest in Greece, have been found incorporated in the walls; another find was the 'Apollonian Triad', the bronze figures of Apollo, Artemis and their mother Leto (Fig. 234).

CASE 157 (BASE). SANCTUARY OF DIKTAEAN ZEUS. THE HYMN OF THE KOURETES

On top of the ruins of the Minoan city in Palaikastro at the eastern edge of Crete, a sanctuary and temple dedicated to the Cretan Diktaean Zeus was founded about half a millennium later. It operated from the 9th century BC until the 4th century AD. Important offerings include bronze shields similar to those from the Idean Cave (Room XVII). One stands out, with an omphalos in the form of a lion's head and an embossed decoration of sphinxes and lions – themes derived from Levantine iconography (Fig. 230).

230

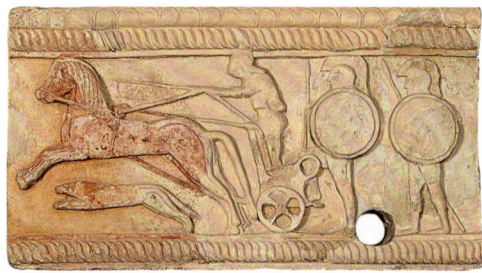

231. Clay plaque depicting a chariot race. Palaikastro, temple of Diktaean Zeus, 6th c. BC.

232. Bird-divine symbols, from poros stone. Amnisos, sanctuary of Zeus Thenatas, middle of the 6th c. BC.

233. The Hymn of the Kouretes. Palaikastro, temple of Diktaean Zeus, 3rd c. AD.

234. The 'Apollonian Triad', bronze statuettes of Apollo, Artemis and Leto. Dreros, 'Delphinion', 8th c. BC.

A bronze mask of the Medusa Gorgon and a Satyr mask are also noteworthy. The *sima*, the edge of the roof that also served as the temple's guttering, consists of a continuous series of clay slabs depicting in relief chariot races accompanied by hoplites and dogs running under the chariots (**Fig. 231**). These are all moments derived from the sports and parades of the martial aristocracy.

A particularly important case is the famous Hymn of the *Kouretes* (**Fig. 233**) engraved on both sides of a stone stele which was found in the same sanctuary. The text, which encapsulates the ideals of a well-ordered state, is a poetic appeal of the city's youth to the 'Greatest Kouros', protector of cities, youth and nature. He is invited to descend with the Kouretes, leaping all the way from Dikti, to listen to their song and bring peace, fruitfulness to the earth, abundant flocks, happiness to the homes, safe voyages in sea, prosperity to the cities and protection to the young citizens. The stele dates back to the 3rd century AD, but it is based on ideals from the 4th–3rd centuries BC, perhaps even earlier.

CASE 158. OTHER SACRED PLACES

From a small sanctuary with a bench in Makellos Kavousi, in a mountainous area which is difficult to access, comes the base of a large clay idol depicting a female deity. Finds from the sanctuary of Zeus Thenatas on the beach of Amnisos, east

of Heraklion, include a dedicatory inscription of the 2nd-1st centuries BC, mentioning the name of the worshiped god, a limestone head-mask, and bronze and faience figurines of Egyptian deities of the 9th–6th centuries BC.

CENTRAL PEDESTALS. THE DIVINE BIRDS

Two large sculptural effigies of birds made from limestone and set on bases decorated with spirals come from the same sanctuary, that of Zeus Thenatas at Amnisos (**Fig. 232**). They depict an eagle and a falcon, symbols of Zeus and Hera respectively. Perhaps they were placed on poles so that they could be seen from afar as landmarks.

CASE 159. THE 'APOLLONIAN TRIAD'

Three small bronze statues (**Fig. 234**) thought to depict the god Apollo, his mother Leto and sister Artemis were found at Dreros, in the so-called Delphinion, which was a one-room temple with a central hearth dedicated to Apollo. They were perhaps placed on a built stone structure along with goat horns and bronze objects. They represent the earliest known Greek examples of a particular type of bronze statue, created by bronze sheets fixed onto a wooden frame, which has not been preserved. They date to the 8th century BC.

ROOM XVI
Geometric, Archaic and Classical Period (11th–4th centuries BC)

TRADE – CULTURAL INFLUENCES

After the fall of the Mycenaean centres in the 11th century BC and a period of relative stagnation and isolation, Cretan merchants made a vigorous comeback on the sea routes in the Aegean and began contacting the Greek cities of central Greece and the East. Relations became even more close during the 8th and 7th centuries BC: vases, utensils and luxury items with special ideological symbolism are now imported on a large scale into Crete. Many local imitations testify to the range of influences, to open communications and cultural convergences. Most objects come from tombs, mainly from Knossos.

CASES 160-163. IMPORTS AND IMITATIONS

Clay and bronze vessels are imported from Phoenicia. One such bronze hemispherical bowl, a handleless vessel from a tomb at Knossos dated to the 9th century BC, bears a Phoenician inscription with the owner's name and patronymic, the earliest known yet in the Greek world. A limestone anthropomorphic and pillar-shaped funerary stele may have been placed on the tomb of a Phoenician merchant who died at Knossos. From Cyprus, with which there were close and frequent commercial contacts from the 10th to the 7th centuries BC, come a series of small anthropomorphic and bird-shaped vases that may have contained aromatic oils as well as many Cretan imitations of such vases, as well as clay tripods that copy the shape of the bronze ones and a stirrup-jar with the 'comb' motif, which had religious significance.

A series of vessels were imported from Egypt and Syro-Palestine. A peculiar case (**Fig. 235**) has the form of a lion holding a hollow cylinder. It belongs to the category of the so-called 'trick vases', because, depending on how it moves, the liquid appears or disappears inside the tubular part. Other imports in faience are an Egyptian bossed bowl (**Fig. 236**) and an ape figurine. Equally interesting are the faience figurines of Egyptian deities such as Bes, Ptah-Seker (**Fig. 237**) and Nefertem (**Fig. 238**). From Mesopotamia comes the handle of a fan and from Luristan (SW Iran) a bronze chest ornament. An askos-shaped vase is of Sardinian origin, while a bronze knife with an anthropomorphic handle shows similarities to a type known from Northern Italy. A series of vessels from Knossos documents contacts with Corinth (**Fig. 239**), Attica and the Cyclades, mainly in the 8th and 7th centuries BC. An impressive East Greek clay cauldron, copying a bronze counterpart, with representations of griffins, sphinxes and goats, as well as vases from Rhodes decorated with grazing goats arranged in zones , testify to relations with Greek regions in the Dodecanese and southwest Asia Minor, mainly in the 7th century BC.

235

CASE 164. HOARDING IN CAULDRONS

Two copper cauldrons from Agia Pelagia west of Heraklion, where the ancient city of Apollonia was located, were found placed inside a pit dug into the rock and covered with a heavy stone slab. Two large holes in the slab corresponded to the mouths of the cauldrons and were themselves sealed with stone lids, which were put in place and removed with the use of straps. Thus, one could deposit valuables inside the cauldrons, but also ensure their safety by placing back and securing the caps. Corresponding or similar constructions found outside Crete also served as 'treasuries' for the safekeeping of high-value offerings.

An inscription cut into the rim of one cauldron – 'Thalios dedicated (it) to Apollo' – reveals the existence of an unknown sanctuary of Apollo in the area. They are dated around 500 BC.

WALL. INSCRIPTION FROM ELTYNA. 'PHOENICIAN LETTERS'

Part of a poros-limestone slab with a very worn and incomplete inscription was found in Kounavoi, in the area of ancient Eltyna; it dates to around 600 BC or shortly after. Provisions of legal content are set out in Cretan Archaic letters, referring to financial transactions. The great importance of the inscription as evidence for the origin of Greek writing is found at the beginning of the second line. Here is preserved the oldest known written reference to the Greek alphabet under the name *'foinikiia'*, i.e. phoenician letters from Phoenicia. The validity of Herodotus' information about the origin of Greek alphabetic writing from the Phoenicians is thus documented for the first time in an actual inscription. The ancient Cretans, apparently aware of this origin, called the Greek letters Phoenician. The opinion of expert scholars that the Greek alphabet was initially formed in Crete is thus clearly strengthened.

235. Faience vessel in the form of a lion, an example of a 'trick vessel'. Knossos, 8th c. BC.

236. Faience omphalos bowl of Egyptian origin. Knossos, 7th c. BC.

237, 238. Egyptian faience figurines of the deities Ptah-Seker and Nefertem. Knossos, 700 BC

239. Corinthian ewer (oinochoe). Knossos, 7th c. BC.

ROOM XVII
Geometric, Archaic and Classical Period (11th–4th centuries BC)

THE SANCTUARIES: FROM MINOAN CULT TO THE AMALGMATION OF RELIGIOUS BELIEFS

Gods with names of the Olympian twelve gods are already mentioned on the Knossos tablets of the 14th century BC (Room IX), but the Greek pantheon as an official cult is only gradually established in the early Greek years, often under the influence of the Minoan past. Cretan sanctuaries and temples never acquired the monumental dimensions and architectural typologies of their mainland Greek counterparts with their surrounding colonnades. In addition to the roofed sanctuaries, worship continues in caves and in the open air, in some cases uninterruptedly from the prehistoric era until the late Roman period, i.e. from the 2nd millennium BC until the 4th century AD.

CASES 165, 166. THE SANCTUARY OF HERMES AND APHRODITE AT SYMI VIANNOS

A typical example of uninterrupted continuity of worship for more than two millennia, from 2000 BC until the 7th century AD, is the extensive mountain sanctuary of Symi. It is located in a pine forest of particular natural beauty in the mountains of Viannos, next to the spring that emerges from the root of a centuries-old plane tree. Its two thousand years of use have left a network of complex architectural remains. In the first, Protopalatial phase (1900–1700 BC), there were hypostyle halls, but in the Neopalatial period (1700–1450 BC) worship was focused on the large, open-air enclosure with a podium-platform inside, accompanied by many auxiliary rooms for housing the priesthood and keeping the utensils. Outdoor worship continued from the 8th century BC onwards with various offerings placed around the altar and on built terraces with retaining walls. From the 7th century BC, the god Hermes was worshiped in the sanctuary, along with Aphrodite, from the Hellenistic period. From the 4th century BC worship was transferred to a single-roomed shrine, which was succeeded in the Christian years by a small church built above the ancient ruins.

Countless votives of all kinds were found in the sanctuary. Associated with the Minoan periods of worship, especially the Neopalatial phase of the cult, are numerous large vessels of the 'communion cup'/chalice type, along with bronze figurines of worshippers and stone offering tables. Donors, who belonged to the palatial court of Knossos, dedicated three long bronze swords with ivory handles and elaborate incised decoration during the Final Palatial period (1450–1370 BC). Similar swords have been found in tombs at Knossos.

Many distinguished votive offerings belong to the Geometric and Archaic periods, which were the heyday of the sanctuary. Among them, one can find models of sceptres, apparently the property of dignitaries, priests or the 'kosmoi', clay masks, relief clay plaques with representations of a female deity, bronze plate models of garments and tributes left by warriors such as model-shields and many arrows. Many of the figurines embody attributes of their dedicators: the musician-lyre player, the shield- and helmet-bearing warrior, the archer-hunter, the young man (kouros) (**Fig. 240**). We even see the figure of the centaur, a hybrid creature with a horse's body and human torso and head. The figures of the cup-bearing man (**Fig. 241**), the self-flagellant, and the pair of sexually-emphasized ithyphallic males allude directly

240

242

243

244

or indirectly to rites of initiation and the education of the young. A series of cut-out bronze plates provides us with accurate images of the initiation ritual, which involves the carrying of goats, alive or butchered, to the shrine by young hunters (**Fig. 242-244**). Representations of the god Hermes, as worshiped in the sanctuary, are shown on other plates: the god is depicted as a hunter-archer (**Fig. 245**), just like the humans, but with winged feet, as per his usual characteristic feature. On another instance, he is depicted as a young beardless man with sceptre and staff (**Fig. 246**), richly clothed and shod. Then again, as the god of trees, '*Kedritis*' (of the cedars specifically) – his epithet according to an inscription found in the sanctuary, a quality that is depicted on a very representative sheet, depicting the god perched in a tree. Hundreds of bronze figurines of animals, mainly cattle, make up the visible manifestations of faith by the shepherds and herd owners. From the later phases of worship, from the 3rd century BC until the 7th century AD, come clay female figurines, lamps and a figurine of Hermes in his messenger guise.

240. Bronze figurine of a young man (kouros). Sanctuary of Symi, 7th c. BC.

241. Bronze figurine of a man holding a cup. Sanctuary of Symi, 8th c. BC.

242-244. Bronze plates with hunters carrying wild goats. Sanctuary of Symi, 7th c. BC.

245. Bronze plate with the god Hermes, shown as an archer with winged feet. Sanctuary of Symi, 7th c. BC.

246. Bronze plate with the god Hermes as a youth with a staff. Sanctuary of Symi, 7th c. BC.

245   246

247

248

CASE 167. THE SANCTUARY OF ATHENA AT SMARI

In a small room-shrine with a bench set within a complex of long rectangular buildings of the megaron type, clay plaques were recovered, depicting a veiled and helmeted female figure, perhaps of Athena.

Two peculiar clay stands from the same sanctuary probably served to support cauldrons. They date back to the 7th century BC.

CASE 168. THE SANCTUARY OF ATHENA ON THE ACROPOLIS OF GORTYNA

The complex of the Geometric-Archaic sanctuary in Gortyna includes many rooms and terraced spaces on the slope of the hill, with a series of retaining walls. A large volume of votives was found in the sanctuary, mainly from the 8th and 7th centuries BC. Among them, we can mention the relief limestone slabs showing the 'Holy Triad' and a seated statue (Room 26, ground floor). Among the many small offerings

249

are bronze models of weapons, clay shields, and a statuette of a female figure, possibly of Athena, along with various types of clay female figurines (**Fig. 247**) be they mortals or gods, a figurine of a ram-bearing man, and an animal carrying a load of wood. Clay relief plaques mainly from the 7th century BC depict the myth of Bellerophon and Pegasus, as well as self-crowning female figures, a goddess with a priestly cylindrical headdress – the *polos*, and even the 'Holy Triad' all three bearing a tall *polos,* as well as mythical beings such as sphinxes (**Fig. 248**). Of interest is the plaque depicting the murder of Aegisthus or Agamemnon, dramatic events of revenge from the mythical Atreides cycle. A large Attic *dinos*, a large spherical vessel of the 6th century BC, is decorated with a black-figure representation of a horse race, where the superintendent of the competition is depicted together with tripods, the prizes of victory.

CASE 178 (CENTRAL). VESSELS OF WORSHIP

Several cult vessels belonging to the kernos type (**Fig. 249**) were discovered in the sanctuary of Gortyna, with multiple bowls for receiving offerings, some with models of a hut on the top, as well as a small clay cauldron with three-dimensional busts of griffins, copying a bronze original.

SACRED CAVES

CASES 169–173. THE IDEAN CAVE

The famous sacred cave on Mount Ida which according to legend was the place of the upbringing of the infant Zeus, was a centre of purification and initiations boasting a widespread reputation and influence in the ancient world. The mystery rites conducted at the Idean Cave attracted believers seeking spiritual cleansing. Prominent spiritual figures of antiquity are mentioned among the sanctuary's visitors: the sage and seer Epimenides and the great philosopher, mystic and founder of his own School, Pythagoras of Samos. Worship in the cave continued uninterrupted from prehistoric times until late antiquity, with a peak period in the 8th and 7th centuries BC.

Representative exhibits from the Minoan period (1900–1450 BC) are a jug, a bronze double axe, a lead talent of the same shape and seals. Most of the votives though date from the 8th to the 3rd centuries BC: fine ivory artefacts, such as anthropomorphic pin heads, bronze figurines and bowls with embossed representations of animals and mythical creatures of Assyrian or Phoenician origin, gold jewellery and gold cut-out sheetwork depicting the 'Holy Triad', ivory seals and necklaces of vitreous materials. A gold coin with the head of Alexander the Great was a tribute from pilgrims from Polyrrhinia in western Crete, as indicated by the engraved inscription on its reverse.

The bronze shields from the Idean Cave are the most important dedications made in the sanctuaries of the early Greek era in Crete. Using the embossing technique and with a style influenced by Assyrian art, they rendered in relief repeated scenes of battles with lions, predatory and fantastical creatures from the Eastern world, warriors and archers and in one case a naked goddess among lions. The compositions develop in concentric zones around a central 'omphalos' or boss, shaped like a lion's head or a large bird of prey. They date from the 8th to the 7th centuries BC.

The bronze 'drum' from the Idean Cave, an object of outstanding importance, dates to the 8th century BC (**Fig. 250**). It depicts in relief a bearded man ostentatiously lifting in his hands

247. Female figurine of the 'Daedalic' type. Shrine, Gortyna, 7th c. BC.

248. Plaque with relief sphinxes. Shrine, Gortyna, 7th c. BC.

249. Unusual cult vessels. Shrine, Gortyna, 7th-6th c. BC.

a subdued lion and stepping on an equally quiescent bull – a dynamic composition symbolizing dominion over the wild side of nature. He is flanked by two anthropomorphic winged daemons who raise and beat drums. In terms of choice of subjects and technique, the entire representation is based on Assyrian art, but the addition of the drums introduces a new, non-Eastern, element: that of the myth of the *Kouretes*, the benevolent daemons who beat on shields and drums in the cave of Ida so that the cries of the newborn Zeus would not be heard by his father, Kronos, who was devouring his children to perpetuate his divine reign. Thus, the central figure of the Assyrian ruler over nature, the '*Potnios Theron*', can be recognized as an early version of the Cretan-born Zeus, flanked by the daemon-Kouretes. This unique dedication with its strong religious symbolism also suggests that musical instruments were played during the rituals, as indeed indicated by the bronze cymbals found in the same cave.

Other valuable offerings made in the Idean Cave also include bronze stands and cauldrons, which perhaps allude to the bath at birth of the divine infant. Many parts of decorated handles, the legs and the body of the stands with a variety of designs and figural representations have survived to this day. From the latter group come images of hoplites, animals, chariots, a woman with a sword and a ship with oarsmen, at the stern of which stand a hoplite and a female figure, which perhaps recall the myth of the abduction of Ariadne by Theseus **(Fig. 251)**. A large cauldron bears an inscription with the name of the offerer: 'Paistos Syvritas dedicated [the cauldron] from the tithe' (i.e. a tenth of a sum acquired from trade or war booty).

250. The bronze 'drum', with relief representations of religious symbolism. Idaean Cave, 8th c. BC.

251. Parts of a bronze stand with a ship, hoplites, chariots and a pair of figures, perhaps of Theseus and Ariadne. Idaean Cave, 8th c. BC.

252. Face of a female figurine. Cave of Psychro/Diktaean cave, 1300 BC.

CASE 174. THE CAVE OF PSYCHRO – THE DIKTAEAN CAVE

The cave at Psychro on the Lasithi plateau is one of the most impressive karst formations in Crete, with rich stalactite and stalagmite decorations. A centre of worship for almost two millennia, from Minoan to the Roman years, the evocative cave was long identified by many scholars with the Dictaean Cave, birthplace of Zeus according to some versions of the mythological tradition. Its heyday is placed from the Neopalatial to the Postpalatial period (1600–1100 BC) and continues into the early Greek years (8th–7th centuries BC). Representative of the worship of the Minoan period are bronze figurines of worshippers, votive swords and knives, bronze double axes, stone offering tables and many vases. A find that stands out is beautiful face of a female figure or anthropomorphic vase with painted facial fea-

252

tures that dates to 1300 BC (**Fig. 252**). Many are the votives dating to both early and late Greek times. These include clay and bronze figurines (**Fig. 257**), a figurine of the Egyptian god Ammon Ra, bronze animal figurines, jewellery, countless

251

bronze pins and rings, tweezers and bone fittings in large numbers, as well as an interesting chariot model. This ensemble constitutes ample evidence of the popularity of the sanctuary, as well as the social range of its visitors.

CASE 175. THE CAVE OF EILEITHYIA IN TSOUTSOUROS

A cave in the area of the coastal ancient site of Inatos, at Tsoutsouros, in southern Crete, was a centre of worship of the goddess of childbirth, Eileithyia, from 1900-1700 BC until the 4th century AD. Worship there was primarily a female affair, focusing on the cycle of procreation. Clay figurines and figurine groups dating between the 9th and 7th centuries BC portray stages of this cycle: from the couple depicted embracing during the act of love-making (**Fig. 253**), to pregnancy and childbirth. This climactic event in the woman's life is realistically represented, with the mother leaning back in the arms of another woman, who presses down on her belly to facilitate the delivery (**Fig. 254**). After the difficult period of pregnancy and childbirth, the woman, now a mother and a symbol of motherhood, is depicted holding the baby protectively in her arms (**Fig. 255**) or letting it rest covered up in its cot. The sanctity of these depictions is underlined by clay double axes, the ancient Minoan symbol.

The sanctuary was also visited by sailors, as shown by the effigies of ships, as well as by pilgrims from Egypt, who brought amulets and figurines of Egyptian deities also associated with fertility, such as Bes, Isis and Nefertem. Gold jewellery, ivory items, scarabs, grooming instruments such as tiny spoons and pins testify to the wealth and social stratification of the worshippers. Of interest is the sheet from a wooden diptych, once covered internally with wax so that notes and correspondences could be scratched into its surface.

CASE 176. OTHER SANCTUARIES

Bronze and clay figurines together with anthropomorphic beings come from two sanctuaries: in the cave of Hermes Kranaios, set in a picturesque verdant ravine with springs in Patsos Amariou, and also at Afrati (Arkades). A clay plaque showing a relief of a goddess with raised arms was found at Mathia and two figurines of a god-

253-255. Figurines representing the cycle of conception and childbirth: a couple making love, a woman in labour at the time of childbirth, a mother with a baby in her arms. Inatos, Eileithyia cave, 9th-7th c. BC.
256. Mitre, a piece of armour, with winged horses in relief. Axos, 6th c. BC.
257. Bronze male figurine. Cave of Psychro/Diktaean cave, 8th c. BC.

253   254   255

dess on horseback, perhaps Artemis or Eileithyia, at Archanes.

Parts of the martial equipment of Cretan hoplites come from Afrati and Axos: a Corinthian-type helmet with an embossed relief decoration of winged horses, a cuirass of relatively small size, perhaps for a child or adolescent, and *mitres*, which were metal armour sheets to protect the abdomen. One has inscribed on it the name of its owner or dedicatee, 'Karanos', others bear reliefs of confronted winged horses (**Fig. 256**) or a group of men holding a trophy, as well as a representation of a tripod and cauldron from which emerges a figure in warlike gear, perhaps Athena.

CASE 177. THE SACRED CHASM OF KYNIGOTAPHKOS

Kynigotaphkos is an impressive cave-chasm in the Psiloritis massif, some 70 m deep. Around its mouth were found hundreds of clay figurines of oxen, a clay effigy of a shield, as well as drinking vessels of the 4th–3rd centuries BC. A patron god of oxen and bulls was worshipped in the sanctuary. In an inscription from the region of Archanes, the Kouretes are mentioned as the patron gods of large animals with strong legs, namely oxen.

CASES 179, 180 (CENTRAL). TWO ARCHAIC FIGURES

A clay figurine of Athena from the sanctuary of Gortyna. She is represented in the *Promachos* posture, that is, as a fighter with helmet, spear and shield. It dates to the 7th century BC.
The limestone head of young person from Axos dates to the beginning of the 6th century BC.

PEDESTAL. AN ALTAR COVER

The large clay conical vessel in the shape of a chimney, decorated with lions' heads, is an altar cover. It comes from the citadel of Gortyna, and is of the 6th century BC.

CASE 181. RELIGIOUS IMAGES.

Glimpses of moments from the religious life of an Archaic city can be seen on fragments of relief pithoi from Lyttos (7th century BC). In the first, a naked man steps out, holding a wreath, perhaps for an offering at a shrine. Such offerings were made at shrines of female deities such as Diktyna, Eileithyia, Europa Elotia and Ariadne. The second fragment depicts a procession of horsemen holding whips. Perhaps their participation in a horse race is being represented.

A large temple built on top of Minoan buildings makes up part of a sanctuary complex in Kommos in southern Crete. Its three architectural phases date from the 9th to the 4th centuries BC. An interesting offering is a cup from the 7th century BC with an incised representation of the wake (*prothesis*), the display of the deceased on a funeral bier before burial, and a race in his honour. Other votive offerings are faience figurines of the Egyptian gods Sekhmet and Nefertem (8th–7th centuries BC), the base of a triangular clay lamp or censer with a decoration of winged sirens in relief, and a wreath of copper leaves and bone beads, perhaps myrtle fruits (3rd–1st centuries BC).

256

257

ROOM XVIII
Geometric-Archaic Period (10th-6th centuries BC)

THE CEMETERY OF THE CITY OF PRINIAS

The settlement of the Geometric and Archaic period at Prinias, identified with ancient Rizinia, is the most fully excavated of that period. The city has a developed urban organization with streets and blocks of buildings, temples with unique sculptural decoration (Room XXVI, ground floor) and public buildings, as well as a large cemetery.

PEDESTAL. THE GRAVESTONES FROM PRINIAS – THE EMPHASIS ON THE INDIVIDUAL

An important find from the cemetery are the burial *stelae* of the 7th century BC: made of poros limestone they were placed as markers on the stone-built rectangular tombs. The figures incised on them indicate the age, social level and rank of the deceased: mature male warriors with shields, helmets, spears and swords, a man enthroned with a sceptre, apparently a city official, a female figure holding a bird and a wreath of pomegranates, a symbol of immortality but also denoting the young age of the deceased, and a woman with a spindle and distaff, the timeless symbols of the weaving housewife. Thus, with simple and easily legible pictorial means, the deceased is individualized and the four main social categories are made obvious: the warrior, the lord-official, the young daughter and the mature female housewife.

CASE 182. BURIAL GIFTS FROM THE CEMETERY OF PRINIAS (8th-7th CENTURIES BC)

Various vases, figurines and a clay model of a chariot (**Fig. 258**), iron weapons, bronze pins and fibulae for clothing, gold jewellery with star symbols, rings, a comb model and a mask come from the tombs of Prinias (**Fig. 259**). All are symbolic references to social status, to the sex or identity of the deceased as members of the society they once lived in.

WALL TO RIGHT. INSCRIPTIONS

The texts of the inscriptions, usually incised on rectangular limestone slabs *(stelae)*, regulated matters concerning the application of the institutions of each city, as well as the life of the citizens. The oldest inscriptions contain legal codes and were placed on the walls of public buildings. The longest integral legal text is preserved in the Great Inscription of Gortyna which dates to the 5th century BC. It is the largest surviving ancient Greek inscription: incised on large poros slabs set in a continuous series and in superimposed rows, it covers provisions regarding public life, civil law and property. It is still located in the archaeological site of Gortyna, incorporated in the walls of the later circular Roman Odeion.

The Museum exhibits other inscriptions that refer to the terms of alliances between cities, such as the one between Tylissos and Knossos, around 450 BC, with Argos acting as arbitrator, which is where the second and most complete

258. Clay model of a two-horse chariot. Prinias, 7th c. BC.

258

copy of the inscription has been found. The borders of the territories are mentioned, while matters of customs, trade, military support and worship are also regulated. Another inscription from Gortyna includes provisions and arrangements for sacrifices and offerings to the gods. The base of a tombstone from Chersonissos refers to the name of the deceased woman, Timo, and that of of Evagros, the person responsible for setting up the grave marker.

CASE 183. THE SHRINE-MODEL OF ARCHANES
This is a small, clay effigy of a circular shrine, within which sits a divine figure with upraised arms (Fig. 260). The entrance is closed by a one-leaf door. On its vaulted roof two male figures, probably worshippers, crouch and observe the goddess through the opening of the skylight. Beside them, reclining is a small animal, perhaps a guard dog. Dense decorative patterns cover all the surfaces. Dated at the end of the 9th century BC, it is the chronologically latest example of the circular shrine-model that has its roots in Minoan times. It was found in the site of an ancient cemetery in the area of Archanes. It is therefore possible that it echoes religious notions of a manner of contact between the world of the living and that of the dead, with their patron goddess present, raising her hands in the typical gesture of supplication and blessing.

259. Gold jewellery with star symbols and a model of a comb. Prinias, 8th-7th c. BC.
260. Clay model of a shrine with a seated goddess inside. Archanes, 9th c. BC.

ROOM XIX
Geometric, Archaic and Classical Period (11th–4th centuries BC)

THE CEMETERIES

From the beginning of the 1st millennium BC the custom of cremating the dead, according to Homeric procedures, gradually replaces interment in larnakes or pithoi. The tombs used now are chamber-shaped, of small dimensions, though small built tholoi, burials inside built enclosures, as well as simple pits in the ground also exist. The largest necropolis of this period is that of Knossos. Other large cemeteries of important cities have been excavated at Afrati (Arkades), Prinias (Rizinia), Kounavoi (Eltyna), Rotasi (Rytion) in central Crete and Eleftherna in the west. After cremation, the bones and ashes were collected from the funeral pyre and placed in small pithoi inside the grave, along with the offerings which comprise jewellery, weapons, bronze vessels and simple clay pots with their contents, all according to gender and social status of the deceased. As part of the burial ritual, dinners took place in honour of the deceased, as well as burnt offerings and libations (liquid offerings) to the dead. The richest burials date to the 8th–7th centuries BC, while from the 6th a period of recession follows, with few goods of poor quality.

CASES 184, 185, 188, 189. KNOSSOS – BURIAL VESSELS

The city of Knossos during the Geometric period is the richest in Crete and one of the largest in Greece, as can be seen from the size and wealth of its cemeteries, from which numerous and diverse burial and ritual vessels have been retrieved.

The pottery workshops of Knossos are distinguished for the quantity and quality of their production, with a vivacity that is clearly visible and is reflected in the products of other workshops in central Crete. Following patterns from the Minoan tradition combined with Eastern influences, the Knossian vases from the 9th century BC stand out through their variety of geometric and curvilinear motifs, the strong influences from mainly Attic painted vases during the 8th century BC, and the individual, locally inspired polychromy used on burial pithoi (**Fig. 261**) from 700 BC – a distant memory of the colour combinations seen on the Minoan frescoes. The fruitful contact with the past is evident in the choice of some figurative subjects derived from the Minoan larnax repertoire, such as the hunt, fantastic winged beings, the variation of griffins, bulls and other grazing animals, birds and the 'Tree of Life'. The representation of a ship is also of Minoan origin, an allegorical reference to the journey of the deceased; the goddess with raised arms also has a Minoan ancestry. Contrarily, a Greek myth is referenced in the image of the god Zeus on a clay lid in the shape of a small shield, holding a bird and thunderbolts in his hands. In front of him is depicted a cauldron, an expensive votive

261

offering in the shrine of the god, below which projects the head of a female figure, perhaps that of Gaia.

CASES 186, 187. JEWELLERY

Jewellery made of gold, silver, faience and semi-precious stones highlight the high social level of the deceased. The material comes mostly from rich Geometric and Archaic tombs of Knossos (Fig. 262-265). A 'hoard' of gold objects, found in a re-used Mycenaean tholos tomb at Teke Heraklion near Knossos, included small gold bars and lumps (Room XXI), as well as other objects, among which stand out two heavy, excellent quality chest ornaments from the end of the 8th century BC. The one (Fig. 262), a crescent-shaped gold-bound rock crystal attachment from which hang three gold crescent- and sun-disc-shaped appendages, is preserved with its elaborately braided gold chain. The other (Fig. 263) is also a gold pendant, crescent-shaped and enclosing a cross of guilloche with small birds in the quarters, heads of female figures at the ends of the crescent, and fine granulated decoration.

From the tombs of Knossos also comes a series of rings, of gold bands sewn onto clothing, jewellery in the form of birds, fish, a panther's mask,

261. Funerary vase with polychrome decoration. Knossos, 8th-7th c. BC.

262, 263. Two ornate crescent-shaped gold pendants. Knossos, 8th c. BC.

264, 265. Gold funerary jewellery in the shape of bees and a man carrying a ram. Knossos, 8th-7th c. BC.

266. Cut-out in gold leaf with a 'Potnios Theron' between lions. Knossos, 8th c. BC.

gold bees (**Fig. 264**) and miniature gold vessels, two small gold images of people carrying rams (**Fig. 265**), as well as silver and bronze pins and fibulae. From the same burial ensembles come a gold plate with representations of men and lions and a cut-out gold leaf in the form of 'Potnios Theron', the master of beasts, between lions (**Fig. 266**). Another object of interest is the Minoan amethyst seal bound in gold, found in a tomb of the Archaic period.

CASE 190. METAL GRAVE GOODS

Bronze vessels, iron weapons and parts of the hoplites' equipment such as bronze greaves have been found in graves. A bronze quiver cover and a votive bronze belt come from tombs at Knossos. The quiver bears reliefs of the 'Potnios Theron' and the belt is decorated with a relief scene of a chariot attack on a shrine with the 'Holy Triad' inside, being defended by archers. The subjects are drawn from Oriental iconography.

For the celebration of dinners in honour of the dead, iron stands were used as supports for the iron *obeloi*, i.e. the spits which held the meat over the fire. A kind of large iron fork would have been used to remove the meat from the spits. These items were found in a tholos tomb in the cemetery of ancient Eltyna at Kounavoi Heraklion and date from the 10th to the 8th centuries BC. Iron spears, swords and knives define the male warrior status. Some swords have been bent over: they were purposely rendered useless during burial, symbolically 'dying' together with their owner.

WALL. TOMBSTONE RELIEFS

The tombstone relief of a 'hunter' (**Fig. 267**) from ancient Apollonia at Agia Pelagia Heraklion is probably an imported work of the 5th century BC, created in Parian marble. It depicts the figure of a young archer with a quiver on his back. The bowed head with its sorrowful face figuratively expresses the pain of premature death.

267. Funerary relief of a young archer. Agia Pelagia (ancient Apollonia), 5th c. BC.

268. Ewer depicting an amorous couple, perhaps Theseus and Ariadne. Afrati (Arcades), 7th c. BC.

269. Vase with a representation in white of a male figure, perhaps the mythical Talos, between sphinxes. Afrati (Arcades), 7th c. BC.

Other tombstones of the 4th–3rd centuries BC show the deceased seated and receiving the last farewell from his relatives, wives and children. The sadness for the lost world of life is expressed by the inscription in rhyme with the words of the deceased on a tombstone from Lasaia: 'Passers-by, you can rejoice, but I leave my loved ones behind.'

CASES 191–194. CEMETERIES OF CENTRAL AND EASTERN CRETE

A series of burial vessels come from the tombs of Eltyna in Kounavoi, Rytion in Rotasi and Arkades in Afrati. The first two sets are strongly influenced by the Knossos workshops. However, in Arkades, the workshop has a rich output, creating a distinct local style by using the black-figure technique and also added white colouring in the depictions of figures and patterns. From the middle of the 7th century BC, vases imported from Corinth and Rhodes reach Arkades as well as Knossos, creating conditions for an interaction between the workshops. Also on display are two ash-urns containing the bones of the deceased after the cremation, and a pithos from Arkades with a representation of a goddess holding stylized trees among birds. A tall ewer (**Fig. 268**) stands out by its depiction of an amorous couple on the neck, perhaps Theseus and Ariadne, rendered with the outline technique; a pithos depicting a rider with his horse also deserves attention. On one vase, also from Arkades, a daemonic winged figure placed between sphinxes (**Fig. 269**), perhaps the mythical Talos, is painted in the added-white colour technique; on another case, the representation of a woman with her hair loose and a hand to her forehead is achieved by an incised outline – she is mourning her beloved dead husband at his funeral. Clay figurines in the form of an owl, a roaring panther and a lyre player, show the typological diversity in the workshop's production. The remains of the bones were placed in a bronze ash-urn after cremation with an *aryballos*, a small vessel for aromatic oils, containing a liquid offering for the deceased.

The clay kernos from Kourtes, with small vessels and human figures applied to its surface, is another case of particular interest.

CASE 195. OTHER CEMETERIES – CERAMICS

Vases and lids with geometric decorations come from other regional cemeteries, such as from the tomb in Ligortynos in the eastern Mesara, and vases together with utensils from Kavousi Ierapetra. An amphora with a representation of a chariot race, a contest in honour of the deceased, and female mourners with their hands on their heads, the commonest mourning gesture in art, is an example that stands out.

268

269

270

CASE 196 (CENTRAL). ANIMAL AND HUMAN-SHAPED VESSELS FROM KNOSSOS: A CRETE-ORIENTAL PHANTASMAGORIA

Clay vessels used for liquid offerings to the dead took the form of animals and birds, or strange, hybrid beings. Most incorporated plastic features derived from Levantine, Egyptian and Cypriot iconography or drew upon narrative elements from myths of Greek origin. The first category includes bird-shaped *askoi*, unusual closed vessels in the shape of a bird, an *aryballos* in the form of a rooster, a sitting sheep and a hare, the open-eyed owl (Fig. 270), another *aryballos* in the shape of a monkey (Fig. 271), a pregnant monkey with an amphora on its head, as well as anthropomorphic vases with upraised arms.

The second category comprises three utensils:

HIPPALECTRYON

This libation vessel takes the form of a daemonic being with the head of a horse, the body of a bird and a miniature rider on the back holding the reins (Fig. 272). The *hippalectryon*, an imaginary being with similar features, is depicted on Attic vases and mentioned in texts of the Classical period. The vessel from Knossos is its earliest figurative version. It dates back to the 8th century BC.

270. Models of owls. Afrati (Arkades) and Knossos, 7th c. BC.
271. Aryballos in the form of a monkey. Knossos, 8th-7th c. BC.

271

272

MALE SIREN

Another libation vessel this has the head of a man and the body of a bird (**Fig. 273**). The siren, a fictional being with the body of a bird of prey and the head of a woman, is an emblematic figure on funerary stelae of the Archaic period. Here it appears in its male form, having a man's head with short hair and a wide open mouth, suggesting the cry of funerary dirge. Beating one's breast, here represented by atrophied arms on the sternum, is also an expression of despair at the loss of a loved one. This vase was found in a child burial in Knossos and dates to around 700 BC.

SIREN-EUROPA (?)

A third libation vessel coming from Knossos has the form of a female siren with a bird's body and female head (**Fig. 274**). However, it displays an additional morphological element that allows a further interpretation. The female element of the figure holds a bull's head, something that has led some scholars to identify the whole as Europa being abducted by Zeus as bull. Perhaps the vessel echoes an early version of the myth, creatively incorporating figural elements of Cretan and Levantine origin. It dates to the 7th century BC.

CASE 197 (CENTRAL). IMAGES – PERCEPTIONS OF THE AFTERLIFE

Objects and models from tombs illustrate perceptions on a deceased person's afterlife. Here, too, the influence of themes on the Late Minoan larnakes is evident: in the clay object from Fortezza of Knossos, we encounter the 'Tree of Life' which is Eastern in origin (**Fig. 275**) and has birds perching on its branches (10th–9th centuries BC). It also constitutes a transference from the iconography of the 'Minoan paradise' as ex-

272. Hippalectryon, libation vessel with bird's body, horse's head and a rider. Knossos, 8th c. BC.

273. The Androsiren (male Siren), a libation vessel with the head of a man and the body of a bird. Knossos, 700 BC

274. The Siren-Europa (?), a libation vessel with a woman's head and a bird's body, ending in a bull's head. Knossos, 7th c. BC.

273

274

emplified on clay larnakes. The overseas journey of the deceased by boat or ship, also a theme of Minoan iconography, is represented as a model of a ship with a human figure seated inside, also from Fortezza at Knossos (7th century BC).

Mixed pictorial elements from the Creto-Mycenaean past are also exhibited on the kernos from Eltyna (9th century BC): the deceased – in the form of a large bird, an allegorical representation of the soul – is the focus of the lamentation of the woman sitting among animals and birds, patterns also known from the repertory of Minoan larnakes. The ostrich egg, a rare grave-good of exotic origin from a tomb in Knossos, echoes notions of rebirth since as an egg, it contains the seed of new life.

PEDESTAL, CORNER. THE KORE OF ELTYNA (FIG. 276)
A stone funerary stele of limestone depicts in relief the figure of a young woman with a faint smile, holding a flower and a wreath in her hands, a symbol of immortality. A Cretan work under Attic influence, it was recovered from Eltyna, dating from the beginning of the 5th century BC.

275. The 'Tree of Life', model of a tree with birds in its branches. Knossos, 10th-9th c. BC.
276. Limestone funerary stele with a relief of a young woman (kore) holding a flower. Eltyna (Kounavoi), late 6th-early 5th c. BC.

275

276

ROOM XX

Classical, Hellenistic and Roman Period (5th century BC–4th century AD)

CITIES AND SANCTUARIES

In the period following the heyday and artistic vanguard of the Geometric and Archaic times, the Cretan city-states consolidated their well-defined territorial and political delineation, with demarcated borders and networks of alliances, as evidenced by inscriptions clearly describing terms and conditions. Gradually, the cities developed broader trade relations with the Greek world and issued coins. In sanctuaries, the worship of fertility deities continued in combination with deities from the Greek pantheon. In Hellenistic times (3rd-2nd centuries BC), Crete was plagued by civil wars, which brought destruction to the cities, constant rivalry and mutual hatred. Finally, in 67 BC Crete was conquered by the Romans. Gortyna, the island's largest city, became the capital of the province of Crete and Cyrenaica. It experienced a period of great prosperity, as did other Cretan cities. Great public works were carried out and magnificent buildings were built, while all art forms were cultivated, especially sculpture and mosaics.

WALL TO THE RIGHT OF THE ENTRANCE.
THE OATH OF THE LYTTIANS: THE DISMAL LANDSCAPE OF THE CIVIL WARS

Typical of the climate of the era of the civil wars is the inscription with the heading 'Oath of the Lyttians' recovered from Chersonissos, the port of the inland city of Lyttos. It spells out the terms of the alliance between Lyttos and Olous, a coastal city in eastern Crete, and dates to 111/110 BC. It has been preserved in three copies: at Chersonissos, Rhodes and Athens, while three more, as the inscription itself states, in Knossos, Olous and Lyttos that have not been found. An important difference in the Chersonissos version from the other two known copies is that the lines that provide for the celebration of the two *euameroi* – 'auspicious days' of Lyttos, i.e. the festive days, have been preserved. These are the celebrations commemorating the re-peopling of the city of Lyttos after its destruction by the Knossians in 221/220 BC, and the anniversary of the destruction of Dreros by the Lyttians. The Lyttians had a long-standing enmity with the Drerians which was matched by a similar 'oath' of the young men of Dreros, who declared that they would not rest until they had destroyed Lyttos, as recorded in another inscription. Dreros was ultimately the loser in the dispute, a fact considered worthy of celebration by the Lyttians.

LEFT OF THE ENTRANCE. TABLE SUPPORT.

Marble table base, in the form of a 'herm' with the head of the god Attis, deity of vegetation. From Chania, 1st–2nd centuries AD.

MOSAICS FROM ROMAN HOUSES

Large Roman villas and city buildings disposed dining halls and living rooms decorated with floor mosaics. Their subjects emanate mainly from the Dionysian cycle, from myths and from comedy plays, as well as images from nature. Two floors with mosaics from neighbouring rooms of a large building in Chersonissos date to the 2nd century AD. One depicts a crater from which grow sprouts with ivy leaves, and the other shows themes from the life of birds in circular frames **(Fig. 277)**. Birds are symbols of happiness and joy, representative of an era of prosperity and cosmopolitanism.

ON THE WALL, projection screen with mosaics of the 'Villa of Dionysos' at Knossos and images of large Roman monuments and portable finds from central Crete.

CASE 198. CITIES

Knossos together with Gortyna were the strongest cities of Crete in the Hellenistic period. After the occupation of Crete by the Romans, Gortyna became the capital and experienced extraordinary prosperity. Knossos, which had put up strong resistance, was turned into a 'colony' and inhabited by Roman settlers from Capua. Witnesses to its heyday are the large Roman Villa of Dionysos with good quality mosaics, as well as many funerary buildings with rich grave gifts (Room XXII). Phaistos was also inhabited after the Minoan years, until its destruction by the Gortynians in 150 BC. Vessels of the 3rd and 2nd centuries BC from the two cities, Knossos and Phaistos, bear characteristic painted and relief decorations.

PEDESTAL IN THE CORNER. ARCHAIC PITHOS

A large pithos from Arkalochori is decorated with reliefs. On the neck is depicted a male figure holding two horses tied with a rope. On the body, a zone with four rams, of which the first to the right has a name in Archaic script, faintly incised before its breast: '*Pios*', i.e. well-fed, fat. The manufacture of the pithos goes back to the 6th-early 5th centuries BC, but it was found in a Hellenistic house of the 3rd century BC.

277

CASES 199, 200, 201. WARS – DESTRUCTIONS OF CITIES

Lyttos, in the central-eastern region of the Pediada, Heraklion, was according to ancient tradition a colony of the Lacedaemonians, inhabited since the Geometric and Archaic periods. A powerful and aggressive city, it had been involved in many wars, particularly with Knossos, which eventually captured it, burned and destroyed it completely in 221/220 BC. A series of vases and a figurine were found in the burnt destruction debris, among other remains. The city was quickly repopulated as the inscription of the 'Oath of the Lyttians' testifies. During Roman times, it experienced great prosperity, as shown by large public buildings, such as the aqueduct and the *Bouleuterion* with its two rows of stone seats arranged axially in the manner of the Roman Curia – the building that housed the senate in Rome and the municipal councils in the provinces.

Coastal Apollonia was located on the site of today's Agia Pelagia, west of Heraklion, in the site of a former Minoan settlement. In the Classical and Hellenistic periods it was an important port protected from winds, with an *Andreion*, well-built structures and craft facilities, such as wine-and-olive presses for the production of wine and olive oil. It was destroyed in 171 BC by the Kydonians. In excavations of houses from the destruction layer of the city, vessels with other objects were found, but also iron arrows mixed with lead slingshots – physical evidence of the violence of the war. Iron nails and hinges recovered come from doors or furniture destroyed or burned as the city was ransacked.

Similar evidence of violence and vengeful fury comes from the charred grains of wheat and the burnt coarse grains from Lyttos. These are the contents of storage vessels that became prey to the flames during the burning of the city by the Knossians in 220/221 BC. The historian Polybius described the dramatic events of the capture of

277. Mosaic with depictions of birds in frames. Chersonissos, 2nd c. AD.
278. Bone bird with its young on its back. Knossos, sanctuary of Demeter, 4th-3rd c. BC.

Lyttos, which was found undefended when its warriors were on a campaign against Lato, its destruction and the enslavement of its women and children.

CASES 202, 203. PRODUCTION – DOMESTIC ACTIVITIES – PRIVATE LIFE

Trade amphorae and stamped amphorae handles from Agia Pelagia, ancient Apollonia bear witness to trade activity with other Greek cities. The pointed amphorae were used to transport wine, being placed in special slots in the holds of ships. Stampings on the handles certified the origin, quality, workshop or date. Cretan wine was famous in ancient times for its quality and healing properties.

Aspects of the daily life of the inhabitants are illuminated by finds from houses, material remains of household equipment and various activities: cooking and serving utensils, sea shells from food debris, mortars for pounding grain, bone pins and tiny spoons that were grooming accessories, loom weights, lamps and chandeliers for lighting at night. Lamps were made in moulds like the plaster casts found at Matala. Hinges, nails, keys and door knockers are all that is left of the metal fittings of doors, windows, furniture and similar utensils.

CASE 204. SANCTUARIES

In the Knossian sanctuary of Glaucos, son of Minos according to tradition, clay plaques were found depicting a man on horseback, the so-called hero-horseman, an iconographic type that appears in various sanctuaries of the Hellenistic period. Similar plaques also come from a sanctuary of ancient Eltyna in Kounavoi. In the sanctuary of Demeter in Knossos, clay figurines were found in the types of *hydriaphoros*, a woman carrying an amphora, and a *Tanagraia*, a figurine of a young woman of particularly refined appearance. From the same shrine come also the figurines of pairs of people, small metal offerings, a silver ring with the name of the goddess and a bone figurine of a bird with its young on its back (**Fig. 278**).

From a large depository at the sanctuary of Demeter in Gortyna, of the 3rd–2nd centuries BC, come figurines of the seated sorrowful goddess type (**Fig. 279**), mourning the abduction of her daughter, Persephone by Pluto, and another depicting the goddess enthroned, as well as figurines of the devotees holding children (**Fig. 280**) and offerings up to the goddess. Large multi-wicked lamps (**Fig. 282**) are probably related to the performance of nocturnal mysteries, the so-called *Lychnokaies* ("Flaming lamps").

CASE 205. PUBLIC SPECTACLES – A ROMAN SPECTACULAR EVENT

Chersonissos on the north-central coastline was inhabited from the Minoan to early Christian times. It flourished during the Hellenistic and Roman years as a port and trade centre as shown by the luxurious houses, the rich offerings in the Hellenistic cemetery (Room XXII), the Roman theatre, the aqueduct, the large water reservoirs, as well as the considerable number of baths.

In the excavation of the city, moulds were found that were used for the production of decorative and commemorative objects in relief. In the matrices, we see the 'negative' of episodes from the popular spectacles –horse races and human-wild animal fights in hippodromes and amphitheatres in the great cities of the Roman empire. Two moulds depict a victorious charioteer with a four-horsed vehicle and a scene of a beast fight where gladiators are spearing lions. Of particular interest is the third mould (**Fig. 281**), the two parts of which formed a three-dimensional model of a ship and other representations in relief. The images refer to a specific Roman spectacle organized in 204 AD by the Roman emperor Septimius Severus. Wild animals are depicted, which were taken to be devoured and killed in the arena of the Roman Circus Maximus, the great hippodrome of Rome. The ship functions here as a representative shorthand, a substitute for the real ships on which the animals were transported from Africa. The constructions and features shown in the mould are meant to be portrayed in perspective, meaning in the background. They are the ones that actually existed on the *euripus* or *spina*, the central dividing axis of the Roman hippodrome: an obelisk crowned by a globe, a mechanism for counting off the seven laps re-

279

280

281

quired for the horse race, columns with statues, a tower and the three poles that marked the turning points of the racecourse. Its rendition is the most complete and detailed that has survived, both of the Roman spectacle of 204 BC, but also of Rome's Circus Maximus.

CASES 205, 206. CLAY AND COPPER FIGURINES
Clay figurines of the 4th–2nd centuries BC come from Agia Pelagia and other sites. Stand-out pieces include busts and heads of women with polychrome jewellery and elaborate hairstyles, a *Tanagraia*-type figurine and an enthroned female figure with a drum and a bowl in her hands representing the goddess Cybele.
The bronze figurines include Hermes with a sceptre, a satyr from the retinue of Dionysos, a female dancer and animals, such as snakes and two mice. Some belonged to bronze vessels.

279. Figurine of a seated and sorrowful goddess Demeter. Gortyna, sanctuary of Demeter, 3rd-2nd c. BC.
280. Figurine of a worshipper with children. Gortyna, sanctuary of Demeter, 3rd-2nd c. BC.
281. Mould for the production of a model of a Roman spectacle of 204 AD in the great Hippodrome of Rome. Chersonissos, 3rd c. AD.
282. Multi-wicked lamps for nocturnal rituals. Gortyna, 3rd-2nd c. BC.

282

ROOM XXI
Classical, Hellenistic and Roman Period (5th century BC–2nd century BC)

CRETAN COINAGE
PRE-MONETARY TRANSACTIONS AND COINAGE IN CRETE

The basic approach for carrying out commercial transactions in the Minoan and Mycenaean periods was the establishment of the relative value of products based on type, material and weight. Metals, mainly copper, and iron, which was introduced from the 1st millennium BC always had a high exchange and commercial value. The minting and circulation of metal coins from the Archaic period onwards was a revolutionary innovation, since the cities themselves provided the necessary certification of the coin's value.

The first Cretan coins were issued in 475–450 BC by Kydonia, a city in western Crete. They were silver staters that copied the coins of Aegina. Gortyna, Phaistos, Knossos and Lyttos followed, also with silver coins, and then most of the other Cretan cities, which issued coins of varying values, with characteristic depictions of mythological themes, symbols and religious figures. Cretan coinage flourished during the Hellenistic period (3rd–2nd centuries BC), with the appearance of series of additional and new mints. With the Roman conquest in 67 BC some Cretan cities retained the right to mint coins, mainly for local transactions. The coin production of the 'Koinon of the Cretans', a federation of Cretan cities that included Knossos, was particularly active until about 150 AD. These are issuances of copper coins, since gold and silver coins were produced by state mints, mainly in Rome. From the middle of the 2nd century AD, only the coins of the imperial mints circulated and continued to do so until the late Roman period, the 4th century AD.

283. Great hoard of hundreds of silver coins, hidden in two vases and buried in the floor of an older tomb. Phalagari Phaistos, 2nd c. BC.

CASE 207. THE PRE-MONETARY ECONOMY

Economic transactions in ancient societies took place mainly on a barter basis: that is, a specific good with a subjectively assessed value was exchanged for another of similar value. In the Minoan palace economy during the 2nd millennium BC, the value and weight of the copper talent, which weighed 30-35 kg, was used as a basis for calculation. Lead and stone weights represented multiples or fractions of fixed units of weight and ranged around 60 grams or half a kilogram, according to weighing canons of Minoan or Eastern origin respectively. The balance for dealing with small quantities of items had the timeless shape of the two bronze circular trays – one for the product and the other for the weights. Scales together with units of quantities of various goods appear in texts of the Linear A and B scripts.

From the Geometric years, in the 10th century BC and later, the rod-shaped iron *obeloi*, six in number – as many as could be held in the hand, initially defined the meaning and value of the drachma, which etymologically derives from the verb *drattomai*, that is, to grasp (the *obeloi*). Another unit was the bronze cauldron, also mentioned in an inscription from Knossos of the 3rd century BC as compensation for harm to animals. A pre-monetary 'hoard' of the 9th century BC was found in vases at Teke of Heraklion: consisting of small bars and lumps of gold, kept together with gold jewellery (Room XIX), it testified that in practice gold has always retained the most stable value in transactions.

CASES 208, 209, 210. COIN-HOARDS

Several hoards of various periods made up of silver or copper coins bear witness to the concern of their owners to hide and secure their small or large sums in times of crisis or war. Most impressive of all is the hoard (**Fig.** 283) of enormous value of about 600 silver coins (tetradrachms, two-drachms, drachms and half-drachms) found inside two vases buried in the earthen floor of a plundered chamber tomb at Phalagari Phaistos. Perhaps it was the treasury of the city of Phaistos, which the officials tried to save hastily before the site's destruction by the Gortynians in 150 BC. These coins of the 2nd century BC come mainly from cities of Eastern Greece, the Aegean islands and Asia Minor, while there are also many issuances by the successors of Alexander the Great. The happy event of this archaeological discovery inevitably means, as in all similar

283

284

cases, that their owners contrarily had bad luck and were unable to return to where they had hidden the hoard.

Other smaller hoards from Classical to late Roman times have been found in various locations in central and eastern Crete. Four silver Aegina drachmas of the 5th century BC come from Knossos and seven silver Athenian tetradrachms also from the 5th century BC from Lato. Hoards of Hellenistic and Roman silver coins were also found in Charakas, Gortyna, Knossos and Sokaras. Hoards of bronze coins have been recovered in various places, such as the bronze *obols* of the 3rd century BC, hidden inside a lamp in Astritsi. The origin of all these coins from cities of Crete, the Greek area and the eastern Mediterranean testifies to their wide circulation, especially of the silver coins.

ISSUES OF CRETAN CITIES

Characteristic coins of Cretan cities dating from the 5th to the 2nd centuries BC are displayed on a wall-map. They usually depict gods and heroes worshiped in each city but also animals or symbols that were linked through myths to local cults, such as the Labyrinth at Knossos (**Fig. 284**) and the myth of Zeus-as-Bull and Europa at Gortyna (**Fig. 285**).

The Cretan 'code of weights' is presented in the exhibition graphically and with examples of the relevant coins. The subdivisions of the basic unit of weight in silver, the silver stater, ranges from the largest, the drachma, which represents half of the stater, to the smallest, the *imichalkos* or 'semicopper,' which is calculated at 1/288 of the stater.

An inscription of the 2nd century AD from Ini mentions wages of persons and value of vessels in dinars and assars.

COINS OF THE ROMAN PERIOD

These fall into two main categories: state issues of Rome and corresponding Cretan coins of the

285

Roman era. The latter, which were minted until about the middle of the 2nd century AD, usually bear Greek inscriptions and figures of local heroes, thus indicating a link to their past.

CASE 211. COINS OF NON-CRETAN ORIGIN

Coins mainly from Greek cities of the Greek world and western Asia Minor have been found on the island, as shown on the wall-map. They date from the 6th to the 1st centuries BC.

CASE 212. SPECIAL USES OF COINS BEYOND TRADE. CHARACTERISTICS OF CRETAN COINS AND MECHANISMS FOR CHECKING AUTHENTICITY

Uses: 1. The *danaki* or 'Charon's *obol*' was the coin with which the boatman Charos (the personification of death) would be paid for the passage of the deceased across Lake Acherousia. It was usually placed in the mouth or hand of the deceased, so that it would not be lost.
2. Coins were used as gaming pieces.
3. Coin types were copied on stamps for the sealing of trade amphorae, providing direct certification of the product's provenance.

Features: Many coins of Cretan cities copy pictorial types and weighing rules from other regions. Their Cretan character is established by references to local myths and cults, through figures or symbols of the gods and local heroes of the cities. The myth of the abduction of Europa by the Zeus-as-Bull, the Minotaur and the Labyrinth (**Fig. 286**) are such instances, as well as the mythical guardian of Crete, Talos (**Fig. 287**).

Verification-certification: This was done through 'marking', that is, by striking a new stamp to confirm the value of the coin. Another method is 'over-stamping', the stamping of a new coin on top of an old one. By incising or cutting the surface in some way, the authenticity of the coin may be certified or its counterfeiting or falsification revealed. If it has been gilded or silvered or if the alloy is poor, the coin is not what it is made out to be.

286

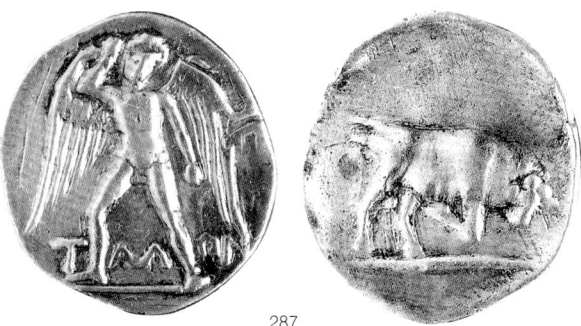

287

284. Silver coin of Knossos, depicting the head of Demeter and a square labyrinth. 3rd c. BC.

285. Silver coin of Gortyna, with a woman in a tree and a bull, referring to the myth of the union of Europa and Zeus-as-Bull under the evergreen plane tree of Gortyna.

286. Silver coin of Knossos, depicting the Minotaur and the labyrinth, mythical symbols of the city.

287. Silver coin, depicting the mythical winged Talos, guardian of Crete, and a bull.

ROOM XXII
Classical, Hellenistic and Roman Period (5th century BC–4th century AD)

THE CEMETERIES

From the classical period onwards, the custom of interring the dead instead of cremation prevails once more. Some rich tombs are marked with relief stelae in the Attic style (Rooms XIX, XXVI). During Hellenistic years, the tombs usually have the form of a simple pit, while in western Crete there are also underground tombs with an antechamber and roomst. Simple pits, built or dug into the ground, covered with slabs or tiles, are common for the Roman period. At the same time, following Roman models, the tombs of wealthy families in large cities such as Knossos and Gortyna often take a monumental form. In the underground type, the tomb was cut out of the rock and provided with arcosolia, meaning arched niches for the deposition of the dead; aboveground, they take the form of a little temple, with a burial chamber. Some bodies were placed in marble sarcophagi with relief scenes, while statues and funerary stelae were erected over the most important tombs.

CASE 213. AN ATHLETE'S GRAVE

Two Panathenaic amphorae from the beginning of the 4th century BC were found in a tomb in Praisos, which on one side depicts the sport of boxing and on the other the goddess Athena Promachos. They bear the expected inscription 'TON ATHENETHEN ATHLON', meaning 'from the games of Athens'. Amphorae of this kind together with their contents, about thirty-five kilograms of olive oil, were given as prizes to athletes who had won in the Panathenaic Games, which were held every four years in Athens. The amphorae of Praisos would have been the prize of the Cretan athlete who was victorious in boxing and were therefore deposited as a commemoration of the victory in his tomb.

288. Black-glaze kantharos with white decoration. Chersonissos, 3rd c. BC.

CASES 214-216. THE TOMBS OF CHERSONISSOS - POTTERY

The Classical and Hellenistic tombs of the coastal port city of Chersonissos contain small vases that are the products of Attic ceramic workshops in unusual frequency. Some characteristic shapes are the *pelike*, a type of small amphora, the *exaleiptron*, the *kantharos* (Fig. 288) and the *skyphos*, types of drinking cups, and the *lekythos*, a vessel with a narrow neck that was used as a container for oil (sometimes scented). They are decorated with simple floral compositions as well as figurative representations, such as a seated female figure with a mirror, a winged figure, a satyr and a maenad, as well as busts of women.

The two marble *exaleiptra* (Fig. 289) – peculiar vessels with a lid and a high foot that were used as cosmetic containers or jewellery cases – are evidence of wealth and sophistication. A series of *pelikes* of the 4th and 3rd centuries BC, imported from Attica, are painted in the red-

289. Marble exaleiptra for cosmetics or jewellery. Chersonissos, 4th-3rd c. BC.

290. Pelike with a representation in the red-figure style. Chersonissos, 4th-3rd c. BC.

figure style (**Fig. 290**). They have representations of Amazonmachies (combats with Amazons), griffins, busts of women, horses and banqueting scenes.

PEDESTAL (WALL). FUNERARY INSCRIPTIONS

Farewell texts in memory of the deceased were carved on stone stelae, which were then put up on the graves. Usually they mentioned the names of the deceased and their relatives. A lament from Itanos for the sudden death and lost life of the young Hexakon particularly stands out: he died at the age of twenty-two and so did not have time to acquire social acclaim. Often depicted are tools, utensils and beloved paraphernalia, identifiers of a profession or status – such as a comb and mirror, an axe, a sickle and a bag probably used for the athlete's discus. They come from various places in central and eastern Crete and date from the 3rd century BC until the 2nd century AD.

CASES 217–222. REFLECTIONS OF LIFE IN THE SCENERY OF DEATH

In Antiquity, death was treated as another, allegorical, aspect of life which continued in another dimension. This perception is expressed through offerings and gifts to the dead, which emphasize the deceased's qualities in life, their social status, gender and preferences, but also include symbolisms on the afterlife,

CASES 217, 218. TOMBS OF CHERSONISSOS AND KNOSSOS

Funerary vessels, lamps and oblong scented oil containers from Knossos and Chersonissos (4th–2nd centuries BC) are displayed here. An egg, a symbol of rebirth, had been placed in a small skyphos in a tomb at Chersonissos. Other graves in the region (late 4th-3rd centuries BC) revealed iron and copper strigils: this is a special tool for scraping off sweat, oil and dust from the body of athletes after competitions in the palaestra and before the bath. Also found were alabaster aromatic oil containers and jewellery such as pins, silver rings and a bracelet, which had been placed on the fingers and wrist of the deceased. The silver coin of the 3rd century BC, Charon's *obol*, was intended for the deceased to

289

290

173

pay Charon to be ferried in his boat to the Other World, sailing across Lake Acherousia. The skull of a very young person is decorated with a wreath of copper leaves and gilded clay beads in the shape of laurel berries

CASES 219, 220. PRECIOUS BURIAL GOODS – JEWELLERY

Valuable grave goods reflect the affluence and cosmopolitan nature of societies during the Hellenistic and Roman periods. Some characteristic cases are the precious rings, such as a solid gold one with the representation of a cupid with a thyrsus, symbol of the Dionysian troupe, and another with a cupid holding a wreath (**Fig. 291**). The gold spiral circlets were used to hold curls of hair together. Silver bracelets with a relief of a female figure and a shield adorned the wrists, while pins did the same for the hairdo. The collection made up of many rings and bezels of gold, semi-precious stones and glass is particularly interesting. They are decorated with engraved figures of gods (**Fig. 292**), heroes and mortals, mythological representations, symbols and animals: Zeus-Serapis, Hermes, Athena, Aphrodite, Erotes-Psyches, Dionysos, Hercules, Centaur, Leda and Zeus-as-Swan, theatrical masks, busts, archers, gladiators, etc. The images render in miniature various aspects of religious and secular life, but also reflect the ambiance of syncretism and cosmopolitanism in Greco-Roman antiquity. The depictions of two ringstones are typical in this respect: One bears the inscription 'Great is the name of Serapis'; its owner would have been one of the followers who worshipped Serapis, the most important Greco-Egyptian god of the Ptolemaic period. The other ringstone has a representation of a lamb, with a cross-shaped sword embedded in its back; apparently it belonged to a believer of the new religion, Christianity. The lamb is an allegorical representation of Christ who was offered as a victim in the sacrifice of crucifixion.

CASE 220

Gold and silver head jewellery and chest ornaments come from graves mainly in central Crete. Their form and decoration drew inspiration from the world of animals, plants and the Dionysiac cycle. The winged Victory earrings (**Fig. 293**) and the fine gold necklace (**Fig. 294**) stand out, while other popular themes are *Nikes* (Victory figures) (**Fig. 295**) and winged cupids, a wreath with gold ivy leaves and silver bracelets with ram's head finials (**Fig. 296**).

CASES 221, 222. BEAUTIFICATION EQUIPMENT

Glass scented-oil bottles (Latin: unguentaria or balsamaria) of various sizes made of pale green or off-white glass were found in Roman tombs at Knossos (1st–2nd centuries AD). The thin elongated glass vessels were formerly called *lacrimaria* because, due to their teardrop-like shape, they were mistakenly thought to have been used to collect the tears of bereaved relatives to be deposited in the tomb. Investigations though have shown that they contained aromatic oils and salves, as well as dyes or herbal mixtures. If the contents had a thick texture, it was scooped out with a thin tool or access was gained by breaking off the neck of the bottle.

291. Gold ring with a cupid holding a wreath, 3rd-2nd c. BC.
292. Gold ring with ringstone depicting Zeus-Serapis stepping on an eagle. Lebena, 2nd c. AD.

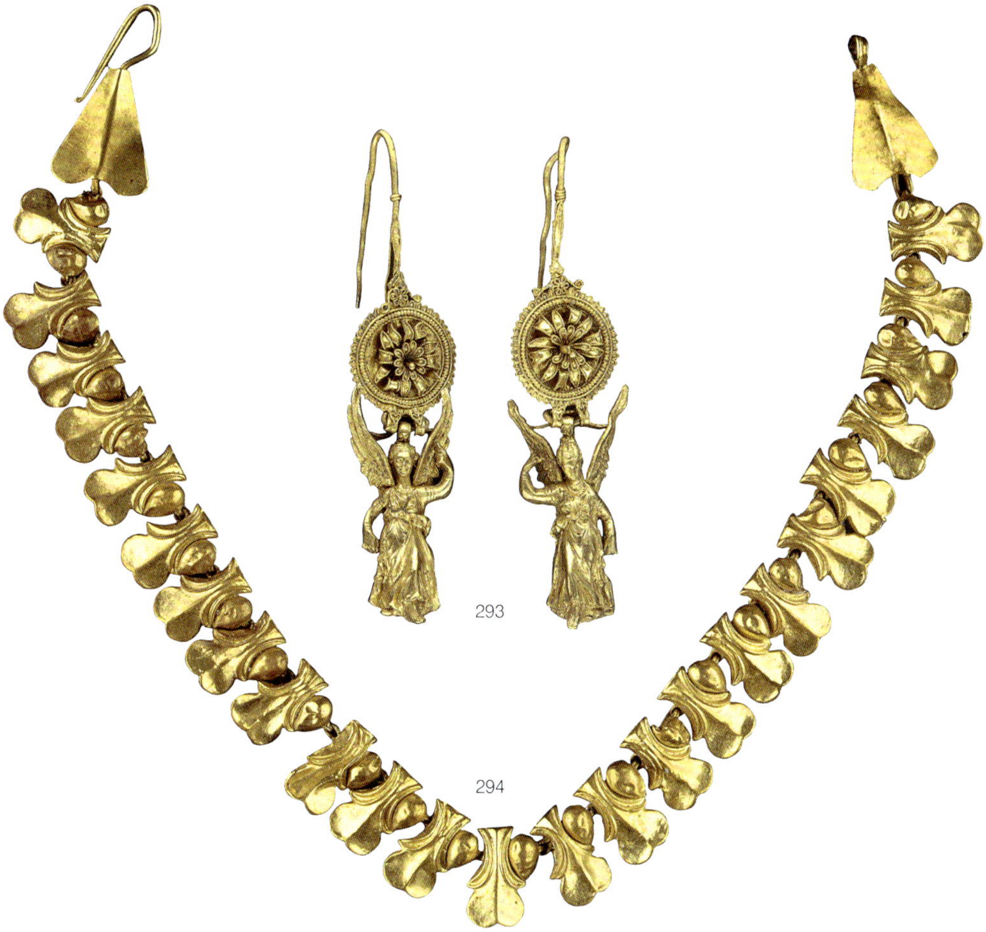

293

294

295

296

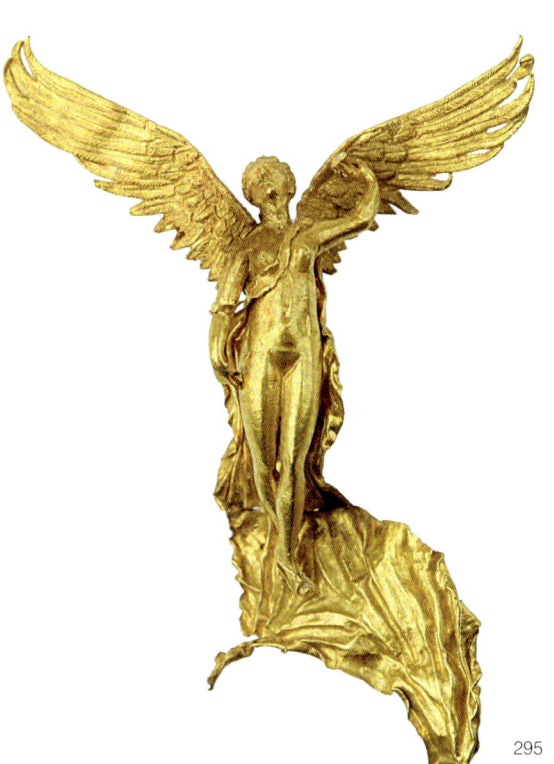

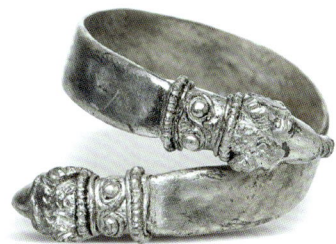

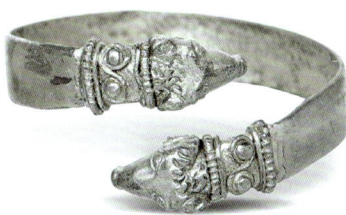

293. Golden earrings in the form of a winged Victory. Kalo Chorio, 2nd c. BC.

294. Gold necklace with beads in the shape of a 'lesbian wave'. Asites, 1st c. BC.

295. Piece of gold jewellery in the form of Victory, 3rd-2nd c. BC.

296. Silver bracelets with finials in the form of a ram's head. Knossos, 3rd-2nd c. BC.

The small round marble pyxides with lids, which served as jewellery or cosmetic cases, were luxury vessels, often decorated with colours, such as the excellently preserved ones from Knossos with patterns in red, green and brown (**Fig. 297**). From Chersonissos come the 'powder cases' (**Fig. 298**), with compacted powder roundels for ladies' face make-up (3rd–2nd centuries BC).

TOMBSTONE RELIEFS AND SARCOPHAGI

PEDESTAL. Marble sarcophagus (2nd century AD) from Heraklion with relief imagery and inscription 'Polybos'. Flute-players are depicted in front of screens, a human skeleton and a table laid with fruits. The basket below it is the *cist*, the sacred vessel of the Eleusinian Mysteries, in which Polybos would have been initiated during his days.

WALL. Tomb relief (2nd–3rd centuries AD) from Gortyna with a symbolic representation of the last journey. Inside the boat that sails swiftly on the waves sits the entire family accompanying the deceased on the overseas journey to the 'islands of the blessed'.

Part of a sarcophagus from Chersonissos (1st–2nd centuries AD) preserves a relief depicting a boar hunt.

Funerary relief depicting a *Necrodeipnon*, funeral banquet from Heraklion (3rd century AD): the dead, just as in their comfortable life, are reclining on couches and enjoying the food on laid tables, while accepting offerings. Their names are mentioned by inscriptions.

CASE 223. SYMBOLISMS OF DEATH

Images and perceptions of the afterlife are provided by the offerings from a Hellenistic period (3rd–2nd centuries BC) tomb at Gortyna. The nuptial *lebes* (**Fig. 299**), a vessel for the bride's bath, is decorated with bas-relief representations of bathing women, figures in tunics holding fans,

297. Small marble pyxis (jewellery case) with painted decoration. Knossos, 3rd-2nd c. BC.

298. Clay small pyxis (powder case), with compact powder tablets. Chersonissos, 3rd-2nd c. BC.

299. Wedding lebes-cauldron with relief scenes. Gortyna, 3rd-2nd c. BC.

300. Winged cupids, symbols of souls. Gortyna, 3rd-2nd c. BC.

men, infants and cupids. They convey vivid images of joy and sociability from the happy life of the deceased to sweeten the pain and loneliness of death. The clay effigies of ostrich eggs from the same tomb are an allusive reference to the expectation of rebirth after death, as are the clay winged cupids (**Fig. 300**), which are symbols of souls and seem to be flying into the tomb.

The Roman lamps from the cemeteries in Knossos, Kavousi and elsewhere, which illuminated the path of the deceased to the other world within the tomb's darkness, are usually decorated with simple patterns. Some carry mythological representations or bold love-making scenes, memories of the intense pleasures of life.

CASES 224, 225. CEMETERIES OF KNOSSOS AND MESARA

Clay vases, clay circular 'medallions' with relief busts of women and a comedy theatre mask of Roman times come from Knossos and Heraklion. The latter perhaps means that the deceased was an actor in life. The tombs of Knossos revealed clay winged cupids with blue and pink colours and a model of the façade of a temple with a triangular pediment and a relief of a bull's head, products of the Hellenistic workshops of Alexandria (3rd–2nd centuries BC). The bull's head refers to the bull-headed god Apis, symbolizing the power of the pharaohs. The gilded disc on the pediment of the temple is the sun disk, symbol of the god.

Hadra-type vases with floral decorations, mainly *hydriae*, come from the Mesara tombs. Their name was acquired from their first discovery in Hellenistic cemeteries of Alexandria in the region of Hadra and that is why they were considered Egyptian. But it was proven that they were manufactured in workshops in south-central Crete and transported to Alexandria.

A *pelike* from Phalasarna at Chania has a red-figure image of an *Arimaspos*, a Scythian warrior on a griffin, chasing an Amazon.

300

CASES 226, 227. INTERNATIONAL TRADE

Bronze lamps of Roman date, whose types were widespread throughout the Roman Empire, are probably imported into Crete from other locations.

Black-glaze and red-figure Attic vases are also traded products, introduced into Crete. A black-coloured vase in the shape of a head with facial features of an African and the black-glaze skyphos with the inscription 'Aithiops', Ethiopian, from the Classical period, fall within the trend of exotic elements of African origin infiltrating Attica and Crete.

CENTRAL PEDESTAL. BRONZE STATUE (FIG. 301)

Bronze figure of a youth in a himation, probably funereal, as his melancholy appearance suggests. A work of high artistic quality from the late Hellenistic or early Roman times (1st century BC). It was found in the sand on the beach of Ierapetra, the site of ancient Hierapytna. This large city in the south flourished especially during the Hellenistic and Roman periods.

301

CASE 228 (CENTRAL). GLASS VESSELS

The technique of making glass vessels is known from prehistory, but glassmaking takes off from the Classical period, going on to flourish especially in the Hellenistic and Roman times. The technique is improved during the Roman period with the invention of blown-glass making. Glass vases of various sizes, shapes, colours and uses, which due to their fragile material are usually best preserved in tombs, make up a diverse and particularly interesting collection **(Fig. 302-304)**. A particular category is the luxurious blue alabastra – scented oil containers **(Fig. 302)** from Knossos, products of the workshops of Alexandria: they are given wavy, polychrome and golden veining (3rd–2nd centuries BC). The decorative birds are also interesting, as are the elegant oinochoes and the tiny coloured bottles for expensive perfumes.

PEDESTAL. ANTHROPOMORPHIC SARCOPHAGUS

An unusually elongated clay sarcophagus, with a specially shaped pocket for the head of the deceased, comes from Lyttos. It is a clay version of the marble anthropomorphic Syro-Palestinian sarcophagus. It is dated in 330-320 BC.

CORRIDOR WALL WITH PEDESTALS.
INSCRIPTIONS OF THE CLASSICAL, GREEK AND ROMAN PERIODS

With the introduction of the Ionic alphabet in Athens, at the end of the 5th century BC, the use of inscriptions became systematized and codified within the composition of the Greek urban fabric. In Crete, the adoption of the alphabet common to the Greek regions takes place at the end of the 4th to the beginning of the 3rd centuries BC. It is mainly used in inscriptions of treaties between cities in the Hellenistic period. There are categories of honorary inscriptions, others of legal and religious content, as well as treaties between cities for peace and alliance. Some characteristic examples are the honorary tombstone for citizens from Itanos (1st century BC), the inscription on the miraculous cures by Asklepios from his sanctuary in Lebena (1st century BC) and a text from Phaistos (2nd century BC) with moral prescriptions governing the entrance of the faithful to the temple of the Great Mother. The alliance treaty of King Eumenes II of Pergamos with thirty Cretan cities, which are listed by name bears importance as a historical document. It includes terms of military cooperation and penalties for violating them. It was found in Gortyna and dates to 183 BC.

Some other interesting inscriptions are a honorary resolution of the Itanians proclaiming as 'consul' Patroclos the Macedonian, sent by Ptolemy II Philadelphos in 266/265 BC, an inscription from the Fortezza of Knossos which refers to the conditions of access to and the keeping of order in the sanctuary of Artemis Skopelitis (1st century BC) and the treaty of Gortyna and Lato (3rd century BC), which refers to a code of legislation, called the 'Diagram of the Cretans'.

304

301. Bronze statue of a youth, possibly funerary. Ierapetra, 1st c. BC.

302. Polychrome glass scent-bottle with golden veining, product of an Alexandrine workshop. Knossos, 3rd-2nd c. BC.

303, 304. Glass vessels of various types from various sites, 3rd c. BC-2nd c. AD.

302
303

ROOM XXIII
Private Collections

THE COLLECTION OF DOCTOR STYLIANOS GIAMALAKIS was purchased by the Greek State in 1962. It consists of objects from Crete and other regions, in Greece and abroad.

CASE 229. EXHIBITS OF PREHISTORIC TIMES. SEALS

The collection includes exhibits from all Minoan periods, which correspond to the ones exhibited in the rooms on the ground floor of the Museum: Prepalatial bone figurines and zoomorphic vessels, figurines from Protopalatial peak sanctuaries, vases, parts of clay figurines and an anthropomorphic vessel from Postpalatial times. Of interest is the bronze double axe perhaps intended as a weapon as indicated by the incised representation of a helmet with a plume on it. A second small one made of gold leaf is similar to the double axes from the Arkalochori cave (Room VII).

The Cycladic marble figurines and the pan-shaped vessel stand out among the exhibits beyond Crete, as well as the Mycenaean small clay figurines.

Minoan seals form an important part of the collection, with interesting examples from all periods. The Prepalatial pieces include one in the form of a monkey, made of bone or hippopotamus tooth. Representations on some Protopalatial steatite prismatic seals reveal the occupations and skills of their owners: a potter with pots and pithoi, an archer, a tumbling acrobat and a ship, the latter referring to the profession of seafarer. The Neopalatial seals made of semi-precious stones depict symbols, religious performances and scenes derived from nature, such as libation vessels, bird-woman and bull-man, bull-leaping, animals at rest or in motion. A special group is composed of Babylonian seal cylinders from the 3rd to the 1st millennia BC and another of Persian seals of the Sassanid dynasty of the 3rd-7th centuries AD.

CASE 230. JEWELLERY

Jewellery in the collection dates from the Greco-Roman era to medieval and modern era. Some stand out pieces are the gold wreath (**Fig. 308**) of large leaves, a gold mask of Medusa, gold rings with coloured ring stones and gold earrings (**Fig. 307**). Byzantine jewellery and other acquisitions from the Venetian and Ottoman

305

306

periods include elaborate gold earrings, necklaces with stones of many colours and pearls, a charm and seals with Arabic script.

CASE 231. GRECO-ROMAN PERIOD EXHIBITS. COINAGE. BRONZE WEAPONS AND TOOLS

The Greco-Roman vases and utensils in the collection include an Eastern-style bronze cauldron (**Fig. 305**) and vases from outside Crete, such as Archaic ones from Corinth and one from Attica. The terracottas of the Classical and Hellenistic periods are interesting, as are the Greco-Roman glass vases.

Coins from Cretan and Greek cities, as well as Roman, Byzantine, Venetian and Ottoman ones, make up a numerically significant part of the collection. They date from the 3rd century BC until the 19th century AD. Some of the bronze weapons and tools date from the Neopalatial to the Archaic era, others are from Hellenistic times. A bronze *mitre,* a semi-circular piece of armour for the protection of the abdomen, bears an incised Archaic inscription: 'Prixus took this' (perhaps as booty) (**Fig. 306**).

305, 306. Eastern type bronze lebes-cauldron and bronze mitre-armour attachment with incised inscription. Giamalakis Collection.

307, 308. Golden earrings and golden wreath. Giamalakis Collection.

THE NIKOLAOS AND THEANO METAXA COLLECTION consists of objects of Cretan origin and was donated to the Greek State in 1997. Part of the Collection is exhibited in the Malevizi Archaeological Collection.

CASE 232. EXHIBITS OF THE MINOAN AND GRECO-ROMAN PERIODS

The exhibits from Prepalatial times include clay and stone vessels of types known from the tholos tombs of the Mesara. Clay vases with polychrome decoration and a two-headed bull figurine belong to the Protopalatial period. The unique clay rhyton in the shape of a ritual hammer and a bronze female figurine date to the Neopalatial period. Bird-shaped vases and part of an Archaic pithos with a pair of heterosexual figures (**Fig. 309**), as well as a bronze *mitre* with reliefs of felines sharing a common head (**Fig. 310**) date to Geometric–Archaic times. The glass vases and the terracottas from Greco-Roman times are also of interest.

BOTTOM ROW. MINOAN SEALS

The number and quality of the seals in the collection, some of which are on display, show the commitment of the collectors to create a quality ensemble, representative of the evolution of Minoan seal engraving. Zoomorphic, scaraboid, cylindrical, conical made of hippopotamus tooth, steatite and white 'paste' with geometric decorative compositions date to the Prepalatial period. From the Protopalatial period come the three-sided prisms and seals of steatite and semi-precious stones with representations of a hunter-archer, animal heads, vases, insects and a cat's mask. Neopalatial seals, lentoid, amygdaloid and compressed cylinders of semi-precious stones, depict imaginary figures such as a bird-woman, griffin, the *'Potnios Theron'* – ruler of wild animals, a lion hunt and religious

309. Part of a pithos with relief depiction of a couple. Metaxa Collection.

310. Bronze mitre with felines in relief. Metaxa Collection.

symbols such as libation vessels, double axe and bucrania. The repertoire is completed by other characteristic patterns of the Neopalatial seal engraving repertory such as animals, birds, cuttlefish and a ship rendered in naturalistic but also abstract style, which is represented by the 'talismanic' seals (**Fig. 313**).

JEWELLERY The collection includes jewellery from all periods, with examples of special quality. Necklaces of various ordinary and semi-precious materials date to the Prepalatial and Protopalatial periods, necklaces of faience and clay to the Geometric period. To the Geometric-Archaic times date silver and gold pins, the interesting small gold piece in the form of a bee, a gold ring with facing heads and a gold pendant in the form of a mask. A gold diadem (**Fig. 311**) depicting a battle between winged imaginary and real beings, gold rings (**Fig. 312**) and impressive gold earrings date to Hellenistic times.

PEDESTALS, CORNERS.
1. Pithos with relief metope-panels depicting horses in a symmetrical arrangement
2. Pithos with relief representation of metope-panels from the legend of Bellerephon. Bellerephon boasted that he could ascend Mount Olympus on his winged horse, Pegasus. The challenge was answered by Zeus himself, who blasted him out of his saddle, causing him to fall from the winged horse and be crippled. The image on the jar depicts the fall of Bellerephon from Pegasus. The myth is an allegory for the divine punishment of human arrogance. Both pithoi date to Archaic times (7th century BC).

311. Gold diadem with scene of winged creatures fighting. Metaxa Collection.
312. Gold ring with head in relief. Metaxa Collection.
313. Almond-shaped 'talismanic' seal of carnelian. Metaxa Collection.

ROOM XXIV, LECTURE AND AUDIO-VISUAL MEDIA ROOM. The projected video displays moments in the history of the Museum: it includes the most important events and persons that determined its course over time. Its story follows the fortunes of the city, from the achievements of peace to the sufferings of war.

ROOM XXVI

Archaic Period (7th-6th centuries BC),
Classical Period (5th-4th centuries BC)

SCULPTURE

Greek art of the Archaic period is defined by the development of monumental sculpted works with clear plastic forms and figures approaching life sizes. This particular stylistic manner of expression during the 7th century BC is called 'Daedalic', named after the mythical Daedalus, a pioneer craftsman and sculptor. Reported in the ancient tradition, Crete's pioneering position in the creation of large sculptures in stone is verified by the formal features of the early Cretan Archaic sculptures of the 7th century BC. Three-dimensional works which were visible from all angles, as well as architectural reliefs for the decoration of temples, figure among the earliest works of this category throughout Greece. Despite their size and rational proportions, human figures are rigid and static. They are rendered frontally, in a standing or sitting position, without a true appreciation of the anatomy and sense of natural articulation of body forms, but with the individual components of the body distinctly shown. A typical feature is the Daedalic hairstyle, the so-called 'layered wig', with its superimposed rows of horizontal curls. Cretan Archaic sculptures, mainly due to the reduced durability of the local limestone from which they were made, did not generally exceed natural size. This may have been aided by a tendency to avoid figures of supernatural dimensions, an echo of the Minoan artistic tradition. From the end of the 6th century BC, funerary stelae are elaborated, according to Attic standards, to mark the graves. After the 6th century BC, the sculptural production is limited and relatively few works of the Classical years of the 5th-4th centuries BC are known. Existing cases – some reliefs and grave stelae – show influences from Attica and the Cyclades. However, the contribution of the artistic tradition of Crete to the formation of Greek art was significant. Famous ancient works were attributed to Cretan creators: the *xoanon* (wooden cultic figure) of the goddess Artemis in Sicyon by the sculptors Dipoinos and Scyllis, disciples of Daedalus according to tradition, or the famous temple of Artemis in Ephesus by the Knossian architects Chersiphron and Metagenes.

LEFT OF THE ENTRANCE. THE FRIEZE AND THE PYLON OF THE TEMPLE OF PRINIAS

This is the decorative architectural sculpture of temple A, the central temple of the Geometric-Archaic city in the area of the village of Prinias, possibly the site of ancient Rizinia.

A series of relief poros slabs, making up a frieze (Fig. 315), are part of the architectural decoration of the temple. We see an array of horsemen in repetitive fashion, on the march with their weapons of war, namely shields and spears. The horses are oversized in relation to the riders, an indication of the animals' importance as a symbol of social class, status and prestige. It surely represents a ceremonial procession by members of the ruling class of horsemen, the aristocratic leading class of the Doric city, during a formal ceremony. The architectural decoration extends to the entrance of the temple and the sculptures that adorned its doorway (Fig. 314). These are displayed by being hung on a modern metal structure in the shape of a pylon, which simulates the entrance of the temple: in the opening of the transom, above the horizontal beam of the lintel, two fully sculpted female figures sit facing each other. They are wearing a high polos on their heads, a sign of divine status. Their clothing bears incised decorations of geometric patterns and animal figures. On the inferior surface of the beam are depicted two

314. Sculptural decoration of the doorway at the entrance of the temple A in Prinias, 7th c. BC.

315. Limestone relief frieze with a parade of horsemen. Prinias, Temple A, 7th c. BC.

316. Reconstruction in drawing of the Temple A in Prinias.

reliefs of standing female figures in an antithetical arrangement, and on the front and reverse sides of the beam we can see reliefs of panthers and deer. The architectural decoration of the temple also includes a stone spiral from the *akroterion*, an architectural fitting that adorned the top of the gabled roof (**Fig. 316**). The sculptures date to the 7th century BC.

RIGHT OF THE ENTRANCE. FRAGMENT OF A KOUROS STATUE

The art of making standing statues of the kouros or kore type (that is, of a young man and a young woman) flourished in other areas of the Greek world during the Archaic period, but it is not adequately represented in Crete. So far, only a small

317. Metope of a temple depicting a labour of Hercules, the capture of the Erymanthian boar. Knossos, 5th c. BC.

318. The 'Holy Triad', a group of deities, two female and one male. Gortyna, 7th c. BC.

portion of the pubic area and buttock of a marble kouros has been discovered. It was recovered at Gortyna, in the Temple of Pythian Apollo and dates to the end of the 6th century BC.

THE 'HOLY TRIAD' AND THE GODDESS OF GORTYNA

Two large relief slabs of the 7th century BC from the temple of Athena in Gortyna belong to the category of architectural sculptures, meaning that they were elements integrated in the structure of the temple. One (**Fig. 318**) depicts a trio of two female figures with *polos*, the cylindrical headdress considered characteristic of priestly status, and a male figure in the centre. The other slab also depicts three deities with *poloi*. The 'Holy Triad' is a combination of figures of religious significance that is encountered in various versions in Archaic iconography.

A poros statue depicting a seated female figure, perhaps resting on a throne set against a wall. The garment is decorated with carved and incised floral patterns and interlocking spirals, accented with red paint. It was probably the cult statue of Athena in the Acropolis temple at Gortyna. It dates in the middle of the 7th century BC.

ARCHITECTURAL SCULPTURES

Akroterion from roof ending. It is made of poros and has the form of the *gorgoneion,* specifically the head of Medusa. It comes from a 6th century BC temple, in the Agora of Dreros.

A poros column capital of the Aeolian type, which belonged to a pedestal on which stood a votive offering. It is shaped like a flower. Afrati (Arkades), 7th–early 6th centuries BC.

A portion of a limestone lion's head from a roof decoration is of interest. Phaistos, 7th–early 6th centuries BC.

A poros relief metope from a temple depicts one of the labours of Hercules: the capture of the Erymanthian boar (**Fig. 317**). Following the narrative of the myth, the scene depicts the hero with the lion-skin across his shoulders lifting the boar on high, while Eurystheus, the king of Mycenae who ordered the capture of the boar, has taken refuge in a jar in fear. Knossos, 5th century BC.

DAEDALIC FEMALE STATUES

The upper half of a limestone female Archaic statue in the form of a kore (**Fig. 319**). It comes from Eleftherna in Rethymnon and dates to the 7th century BC. The garment is decorated with incised rosettes. The elaborate 'daedalic' hairdo is impressive, and is best preserved at the back. The upper half of a worn oversized female statue of the Archaic period (7th century BC) was found in Astritsi. The characteristic 'Daedalic' hairdo, like a wig, is reminiscent of Egyptian statuary. It may have stood on a temple wall, as shown by the holes in the back for its fixing.

A limestone relief plaque (7th century BC) from the mountainous Malles area, this depicts a female figure seated on a throne.

The upper torso of a very worn female statue with a 'Daedalic' headdress comes from Prinias (7th century BC).

A FUNERARY RELIEF

A large marble tombstone (**Fig. 320**) of the middle of the 4th century BC from Heraklion, showing in relief a scene, where members of the dead man's family bid him farewell. The married couple parts with a handshake, a common gesture on tomb reliefs, which emphasizes the separation, but also the bond between the two persons depicted. The woman holds a jewellery case and the little boy the wooden-and-wax board for writing at school, and an aryballos, containing the oil for anointing the body before gymnastic exercises. The work is part of the Attic tradition of funerary stelae, both in terms of theme and style.

319

320

319. Limestone statue of a young woman (kore) in the 'Daedalic' style. Eleftherna, 7th c. BC.

320. Relief tombstone with a scene of farewell to the deceased. Heraklion, 4th c. BC.

ROOM XXVII

Hellenistic Period (3rd-2nd centuries BC),
Roman Period (1st century BC-4th century AD)

SCULPTURE

Hellenistic sculpture is represented in Crete by a relatively small number of works, which follow well-known artistic models from the Greek world, just as during the previous Classical period. However, during the Roman period, sculptural art flourished following two dominant trends: on the one hand the copying and reproduction of famous works by renowned sculptors of the Classical and Hellenistic periods; and on the other, the original creation or import of portraits and figures of members of the imperial families or local officials and individuals. The basic reason for this popularity was the intense classicism adopted by the leading ranks of the empire transplanted to Crete. Consequently, there was an increasing demand for the decoration of luxurious mansions and imposing public buildings or spaces by the rich Romans as well as by the natives, who had accumulated wealth by exploiting the island's key position within the vast Roman Empire. Most of the works date to the three imperial centuries, 1st–3rd centuries AD, a period of prosperity and intense building activity in Crete, during which large public and private projects were implemented, adorned with many marble statues.

SECTION I (LEFT). GODS AND HEROES, MYTHOLOGICAL SUBJECTS, ALLEGORICAL FIGURES

CENTRAL EXHIBIT (ACROSS THE ENTRANCE). STATUE COMPLEX OF ISIS-PERSEPHONE AND SERAPIS-PLUTO WITH THE THREE-HEADED DOG CERBERUS (FIG. 321).

This group complex is a typical example of Greco-Egyptian syncretism in the field of religion. The gods are depicted with symbols characteristic of their identity: Serapis, as patron of agricultural production, carries on his head the *modios*, a vessel and unit of grain measurement. Isis has the disc of the moon on her forehead and holds the sistrum, an Egyptian musical instrument.

The worship of Serapis, a Greco-Egyptian deity, was established during the Ptolemaic period. It combines the names and attributes of two gods, Osiris, god of fertility and the dead, and Apis, the bull-shaped god of Memphis, who was a symbol of strength and masculinity and, by connotation, the power of the pharaohs. Osiris-Apis (Serapis) immediately shed his Egyptian morphological features under the influence of the Hellenistic environment of Egypt. Thus, his iconography was modelled on the standard works of Greek sculpture of the 5th century BC based on the formal characteristics of Zeus. He is sometimes identified with Pluto, god of Hades, and is accompanied by the guardian of Hades, the three-headed dog Cerberus.

Isis, the great Egyptian goddess of fertility and family, is also a protector of the throne. Although a purely Egyptian deity, she too has acquired Greek characteristics, based on a Greek work of sculpture of the 3rd century BC. Her coexistence with Serapis-Pluto and Cerberus here indicates her additional, 'Greek' status as Persephone, wife of Pluto and daughter of the goddess Demeter. The complex was found in the temple of the Egyptian Deities in Gortyna and dates to the middle of the 2nd century AD.

321. Isis-Persephone and Serapis-Pluto, with the three-headed dog Cerberus. Complex of statues of deities displaying mixed Greco-Egyptian features and symbols, an example of the religious syncretism that took shape in the complex cultural environment of Ptolemaic Alexandria. Gortyna, Temple of the Egyptian Deities, 2nd c. AD.

GORTYNA

Among the powerful cities of historical times, Knossos, Lyttos, Prinias, Praisos and others, Gortyna occupies a prime position. Already a strong city in the Geometric and Archaic periods (8th–6th centuries BC), Gortyna was then actively involved in the disputes between the Cretan cities, especially with Knossos in the following periods (5th–2nd century BC). Gortyna once again experienced particular prosperity during the Roman period (1st century BC–4th century AD), when the city emerged as the capital of the province of Crete and Cyrenaica. Imposing public buildings and temples were erected, such as the Praetorium, the temple of Pythian Apollo, the temple of the Egyptian Gods (Iseion), the Odeion (Fig. 322), theatres, amphitheatres, the Nymphaeum, amongst others –all adorned with numerous statues. A reflection of Gortyna's power in its centuries-long history is provided by important exhibits of the Museum: relief plaques, ritual utensils and the relief poros slabs with the 'Holy Triad' from the Archaic sanctuary of Athena on the city's acropolis (Rooms XVII and XXVI). Also, tomb offerings, inscriptions and a series of statues from the Roman period stand out, among them the Serapis-Isis complex (Rooms XXII and XXVII). The large and earliest excavations in Gortyna were carried out by the Italian Archaeological School, while in recent years they have also been conducted by the Ephorate of Antiquities of Heraklion.

322. Ancient Gortyna, the Odeion. On the left is the newer building where the Great Inscription is housed.

323. Relief of the intercourse of Leda and Zeus-as-Swan, in the presence of Eros. Knossos, 1st-2nd c. AD.

LEFT OF THE ENTRANCE. RELIEFS WITH THEMES FROM MYTHOLOGY

Double-faced four-sided stele made of poros limestone with relief depictions of mythological episodes: the infant Heracles strangling the snakes, Atlas supporting the firmament on his shoulders and Prometheus bound on a rock with the bird of prey beside him. The stele is crowned by two antithetically positioned heads of a young and mature bearded man that support a basket with relief leaves. Knossos, 1st–2nd centuries AD.

THE INTERCOURSE OF LEDA WITH ZEUS-AS-SWAN (FIG. 323).

A favourite theme in antiquity appearing in many myths is the loves and transformations of Zeus. Here is depicted, in the presence of a small winged eros, the intercourse of Zeus, transformed into a majestic swan, with Leda, who arcs her body and lifts her face with a voluptuous but also ecstatic expression. The fruit of their union were the Dioscuri (Castor and Polydeuces) and Fair Helen, who became the cause of the Trojan War. Knossos, 1st–2nd century AD.

THE TUG-OF-WAR BETWEEN EROS AND ANTEROS allegorically represents the conflict between heterosexual and homosexual or unrequited love. Knossos, 2nd century AD.

THE GRIEVING GODDESS DEMETER is depicted as a seated mourner, bowed head in her hand, mourning the abduction of her daughter, Persephone, by Pluto, the god of Hades. In her other hand she holds the horn of Amaltheia, a symbol of the fertile and bountiful earth, which refers to her main attribute as the goddess of agriculture, vegetation and fertility. Knossos, 1st–2nd centuries AD.

323

GODS OF THE OLYMPIAN PANTHEON

ARTEMIS AIMS HER ARC AT THE CHILDREN OF NIOBE

A composition of small statues (**Fig. 324**) of the middle of the 2nd–3rd centuries AD from Inatos, depicts the vengeful slaying of Niobe's children by the goddess Artemis. According to legend, Niobe boasted that she had fourteen children, while Leto, mother of Artemis and Apollo, had only two. Thus, she incurred the wrath of the fraternal divine couple who killed all her children. Here Niobe is depicted trying in vain to protect her child, while Artemis, dressed in a short tunic and hunting boots, shoots it down. This group is one of the most complete surviving copies of an original work from the 4th century BC, that of a famous sculptor, possibly Scopas or Praxiteles.

ASPECTS OF APHRODITE

Statues of Aphrodite were extremely popular during the Roman period. They reproduced famous original sculptures from the Classical period. They graphically depict admiration for female beauty and a penchant for voluptuousness.

STATUE OF APHRODITE OR A NYMPH (**Fig. 325**) holding a basin. The rendering of the face is excellent, echoing a classical model of the 4th century BC. Gortyna, 1st century AD.

STATUE OF APHRODITE, OF THE SO-CALLED GENETRIX TYPE. Copy of an original work of the end of the 5th century BC by the sculptor Callimachos. A morphological and stylistic feature of the period of the original piece is the 'wet', transparent tunic that traces the body underneath and leaves one breast bare. Gortyna, 1st–2nd centuries AD.

STATUE OF NAKED APHRODITE (**Fig. 326**) is in the '*squatting*' type, namely almost seated, but with one leg bent in a kneeling position. This is a copy of a bronze original of the 3rd century BC made by sculptor Doidalsas. Gortyna, early 2nd century AD.

324

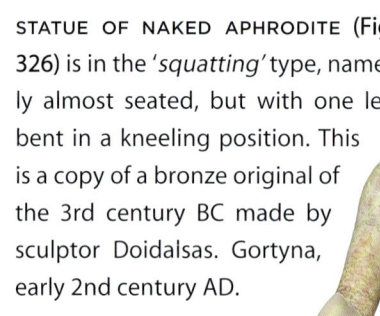

325

SMALL STATUE OF NAKED APHRODITE close to the type of the so-called Knidian Aphrodite, which was a famous work of the 4th century BC made by sculptor Praxiteles. Gortyna, 1st century AD.
STATUE OF THE GODDESS APHRODITE, copy of a work of the 5th century BC, attributed to the sculptor Alkamenes, a pupil of Pheidias. It became known as 'Aphrodite in the Gardens' from the verdant 'Gardens' site in ancient Athens, where it was installed. Gortyna, 2nd-3rd centuries AD.
STATUE OF HALF-NUDE APHRODITE AND SMALL NUDE APHRODITE STATUE from Gortyna and Knossos respectively, 1st–2nd centuries AD.
HEAD OF APHRODITE STATUE (Fig. 327) Gortyna, 1st century AD.

STATUE OF ATHENA PARTHENOS: Roman copy in the type of the famous colossal chryselephantine statue of Athena Parthenos, the work of the great sculptor Pheidias of the 5th century BC. The prototype was the cult statue of the goddess inside the Parthenon, a leading symbol of the heyday of the Athenian democracy and an object of admiration throughout the ancient world. Gortyna, 2nd century AD.

STATUE OF HERMES KERDOOS (PROFIT-BEARER), the patron god of trade and profitability. His symbol is the *valantion*, the coin pouch. Gortyna, 1st-2nd century AD.

OTHER GODS OF THE GREEK PANTHEON.
ALLEGORICAL FORMS AND MYSTICS

TWO BUSTS OF THE GOD DIONYSOS: In one case the god is depicted beardless (Fig. 328), and in the other he has small horns and a wreath of ivy and grapes. Knossos and Plora respectively, 2nd century AD.
SMALL STATUE OF THE GOD DIONYSOS (Fig. 329) wearing long tunic and *himation*, a kind of cloak. On his head he carries a wreath of ivy leaves and pine cones. The statue belongs to the so-called 'Sardanapalus' type, a work of Praxiteles around 300 BC. Knossos, 2nd–3rd centuries AD.

326

327   328

324. The goddess Artemis aiming her bow at the children of Niobe. Inatos, 2nd c. AD.
325. Statue of Aphrodite or Nymph. Gortyna, 1st c. AD.
326. Aphrodite "Oklazousa", in a squatting posture, Gortyna, 2nd c. AD.
327. Head of statue of Aphrodite. Gortyna, 1st c. AD.
328. Protome of the god Dionysus. Knossos, 2nd c. AD.

TWO STATUES OF THE GOD PAN (Fig. 330) The goat-formed god was a protector of shepherds and a follower of Dionysos. His symbols are the ram and the animal skin over the shoulder, as well as the pan-pipes, a musical wind instrument made of reeds. He figuratively expresses the primordial fertilizing powers of nature. Argyroupolis (ancient Lappa) and Gortyna, 2nd century AD.

SMALL STATUE OF PEACE holding in her arms the infant *Pluto* (Wealth). This is copy of a well-known work of the 4th century BC of the sculptor Kiphisodotos. It is an allegory for the wealth that grows during a time of peace. Knossos, 2nd century AD.

STATUE OF THE PUDICITIA TYPE, an allegorical expression of *Aidos*, female modesty and decency. Knossos, 2nd century AD.

STATUE OF THE GODDESS HYGEIA – HEALTH, the daughter of Asklepios, with the symbol of the snake. Her worship became particularly popular in the Hellenistic period. Lyttos, 2nd century AD.

HEADLESS STATUE OF A GOD with mixed features of Egyptian and Greek deities. His posture is typical of the god Osiris. He holds a sceptre with lotuses, while a serpent coils around his torso, a symbol of Asklepios or Zeus. His clothing is decorated with stars, a typical symbol of the god of astronomy, Imhotep – Imouthis to the Greeks, as is the notebook on his left shoulder. It is dated to the 1st–2nd centuries AD.

STATUE OF A MUSE with a 'transparent' tunic covering the body in imitation of the 'wet style', a look of the late 5th-early 4th centuries BC. It is dated to the 1st-2nd centuries AD.

STATUE OF POTHOS, A PERSONIFICATION OF LUST. A good quality, yet fragmentary, copy of a well-known work by the sculptor Skopas, dating to the 4th century BC. Pothos, the son of Aphrodite and Eros, is an allegorical expression of amorous desire that is graphically portrayed in his relaxed, sensual pose. His tunic rests on a goose, Aphrodite's favourite bird. Gortyna, 1st–2nd centuries AD.

STATUE OF A PHILOSOPHER (Fig. 331) This shows a mature bearded man of the *peripatetic* philosopher type, with staff in hand and bundle of books by his left foot. It probably depicts the eminent Neo-Pythagorean philosopher Apollonios Tyanaeus, teacher, physician and mystic of the 1st century AD, with a great reputation as a healer and miracle worker in the Greco-Roman, and even, later on, in the Arab world. He also toured Crete where he taught in Gortyna and Lebena. He is said to have died in the sanctuary of Diktynna in western Crete. Gortyna, end of the 2nd–beginning of the 3rd centuries AD.

THREE BUSTS OF BEARDED MEN of the philosopher, priest or official type. Gortyna and Lyttos, 2nd–3rd centuries BC.

SMALL STATUES OF GODS
STATUETTE OF ARTEMIS in her 'Artemis of Versailles' type. A copy of the work of the sculptor Leochares of the 4th century BC. Gortyna, 2nd century AD.

STATUE OF POSEIDON (Fig. 332) of the 'Lateran' type. The god is depicted leaning forward, resting his hand on his thigh, over which his folded robe is draped. Knossos, 2nd century AD.

STATUE OF ASKLEPIOS, god of health. Gortyna, 2nd century AD.

332

SECTION II (RIGHT OF THE ENTRANCE). STATUES OF MORTALS. FUNERARY RELIEFS

The statues and portraits realistically depict figures of emperors, officials, athletes, members of imperial families, and of the aristocracy; they are often based on earlier works by famous sculptors. The tomb reliefs represent scenes of everyday life, while there are also some allegorical representations.

LARGE MARBLE SARCOPHAGUS (Fig. 333) with rich relief decoration. Themes of an apocalyptic character and symbolism that refer to the regeneration of life often decorate sarcophagi of the Greco-Roman era: cupids holding garlands of leaves and fruits, heads of Medusa, bucrania, heads of lions. The sarcophagus was found in Malia, under the Holy Altar of a Christian church, and the bones it contained may have belonged to martyrs or other holy figures blessed of the church. Inside were found gold jewellery exhibited in Room XXII. It dates to the 3rd century AD.

329. Small statue of Dionysos-'Sardanapalus'. Knossos, 2nd-3rd c. AD.
330. Statue of the goat-footed god Pan holding a syrinx (pipe). Argyroupolis (ancient Lappa), 2nd c. AD.
331. Statue of a philosopher, perhaps the Neo-Pythagorean Apollonius Tyanaeus. Gortyna, 2nd-3rd c. AD.
332. Small statue of the god Poseidon of the so-called Lateran type. Knossos, 2nd c. AD.

SMALL RELIEF FUNERARY STELAE. One depicts a warrior and probably his slave. It was found in Gortyna and dates to the 3rd-2nd centuries BC. The second shows a farewell scene between a seated woman and a standing man. It dates to the 2nd century AD. The third depicts a horseman conversing with a standing man, and is of the 1st–2nd centuries AD.

THE *DORYFOROS* (SPEAR-CARRIER). Torso of a male statue, a good quality copy of the *Doryforos* (Spear-carrier) (**Fig. 334**), a famous work of the classical period of the 5th century BC, attributed to the great sculptor Polykleitos. It depicts a naked man with a spear on his shoulder. It is considered one of the masterpieces of Classical statuary, an original that embodies the principles of proportion, symmetry and balanced movement of the torso and limbs, which make up the famous 'Canon' of Polykleitos. Gortyna, 2nd century AD.

334

333. Large marble sarcophagus with relief decoration of symbolic meaning. Malia, 3rd c. AD.
334. Copy of the 'Doryforos' – the Spear-carrier, a famous work by Polykleitos. Gortyna, 2nd c. AD.

335. Statue of a youth in the type of an athlete. Chersonissos, 1st c. AD.
336. Statue of a Roman lady of the 'Great Herakleiotissa' type. Chersonissos, 2nd c. AD.

333

STATUE OF A YOUNG MAN (Fig. 335), depicting an eminent member of the society of Chersonissos or Rome, with idealized features after the type of the athlete. Chersonissos, 1st century AD.

STATUE OF A MAN IN A *HIMATION* (CLOAK), possibly an honorary statue, with a hairstyle from the period of Trajan. Chersonissos. 2nd century AD.

TWO ROMAN LADIES. Two larger-than-life-size Roman female statues show different stylistic features. The Roman mistress (Fig. 336) from Chersonissos in central Crete wears a *chiton* and *himation*, the latter covering the whole body and the back of the head; she has an elaborate hairdo rising off the forehead like tall diadem. It is a copy of the 2nd century AD in the type of the 'Great Herakleiotissa', an original work of 320 BC attributed to the great sculptor of classical antiquity, Praxiteles.

The conventional name 'Great Herakleiotissa' was given because the best-known statue of this

335

336

197

337

type, as well as the smaller counterpart, the 'Little Herakleiotissa', was found in the 18th century in Heraklion (Herculaneum) in southern Italy.

The statue of a young woman, from Kastelli Kissamos in western Crete, this represents a Roman-era artistic tendency to imitate archaic models. The simple vertical folds of the garment, reminiscent of the flutes of a Doric column, give the statue an archaistic look. It dates to the 2nd century AD.

HEADLESS STATUE OF HADRIAN (117-138 AD) **(Fig. 337)**, the philhellene, humanist and philosopher emperor. He wears a ceremonial cuirass with a representation of the myth of the beginnings of Rome, with Romulus and Remus suckling from the she-wolf; a portrait of Medusa the Gorgon and Victories crowning Pallas Athena stepping on fallen barbarians. Knossos, 2nd century AD.

WALL NICHES, FROM THE RIGHT. THE ART OF PORTRAITURE

The original artistic contribution by Rome to the field of sculpture is the art of the portrait. The forms are rendered with individualizing features, without idealization and embellishment. The portrait captures the figures of emperors, prominent officials and private individuals in a realistic manner. Imperial portraits in particular present the emperor as a sovereign ruler at milestone events in his life, such as his accession to the throne, his anniversary, marriage, military successes and in the highest religious office of high priest. From places of worship and honour of the Roman emperors come a series of portraits, detached from their bodies; the statues were originally put up in temples or public places. The Museum's collection includes portraits of Augustus, the first Roman emperor (27 BC–14 AD), Tiberius (14–37 AD), Caligula (37–41 AD), of Trajan (98–117 AD) **(Fig. 338)**, Hadrian (117–138 AD), Antoninus

Pius (138–161 AD), Marcus Aurelius **(Fig. 339)** (161–180 AD), Caracalla (211–217 AD), as well as of members of their families.

Next come portraits of men and women **(Fig. 340, 341)** of various ages and social classes, either relatives of emperors and officials or private Roman citizens. Some, detached from funerary statues, present individual features and elaborate hairstyles following the fashions of each era. Most date from the 1st to the 3rd centuries AD.

337. Statue of the emperor Hadrian with a ceremonial cuirass in relief. Knossos, 2nd c. AD.

338. Portrait of the emperor Trajan. Lyttos, 2nd c. AD.

339. Portrait of the emperor Marcus Aurelius. Gortyna, 2nd c. AD.

340, 341. Portraits of a woman with her hair in a bun and a young man with straight hair. Chersonissos, 2nd c. AD.

SELECTED BIBLIOGRAPHY

Alexiou Stylianos, *Μινωικός Πολιτισμός*, Ηράκλειο 1964

Andreadaki-Vlazaki Maria, Rethemiotakis Giorgos, Dimopoulou-Rethemiotaki Nota (eds.), *From the Land of the Labyrinth: Minoan Crete 3000-1100 BC.*, A.S.Onassis Public Benefit Foundation in collaboration with Greek Ministry of Culture, New York 2008

Betancourt Philip, *The History of Minoan Pottery*, Princeton 1985

Dimopoulou Nota, *The Archaeological Museum of Herakleion*, Latsis I.S. Foundation, The Cycle of Museums, Athens 2005, hppps:www.latsis-foundation.org, e-library

Dimopoulou Nota and Rethemiotakis Yorgos, *The Ring of Minos and Gold Minoan Rings. The Epiphany Cycle*, Athens 2004

Evans Arthur, *The Palace of Minos at Knossos*, I-IV, London 1921-1935

Hood Sinclair, *The Minoans: Crete in the Bronze Age*, London 1971

Kanta Athanasia and Davaras Kostis, *Ελουθία Χαριστήιον. Το ιερό σπήλαιο της Ειλειθυίας στον Τσούτσουρο*, Ηράκλειο 2011

Karetsou Alexandra, Andreadaki-Vlazaki Maria, Papadakis Nikos, *Crete-Egypt: Three Thousand Years of Cultural Links* (Catalogue, Essays), Herakleion 2000

Krzyszkowska Olga, *Aegean Seals: An Introduction*, London 2005

Lempessi Angeliki, *Το Ιερό του Ερμή και της Αφροδίτης στη Σύμη Βιάννου 1. Χάλκινα Κρητικά Τορεύματα*, Αθήνα 1985

Macdonald Colin F., *Knossos*, London 2005

Mandalaki Stella and Rethemiotakis Giorgos (eds.), *The Minoan World: Journey to the Origins of Europe*, Heraklion 2015

Marinatos Nanno, *Minoan Religion: Ritual, Image and Symbol*, Columbia 1993

Momigliano Nicoletta, *In Search of the Labyrinth: The Cultural Legacy of Minoan Crete*, London 2020

Panagiotakis Nikolaos (ed.), *Κρήτη: Ιστορία και Πολιτισμός*, Ηράκλειο 1987

Platon Nikolaos, *Ζάκρος. Το Νέον Μινωικόν Ανάκτορον*, Αθήναι 1974

Rethemiotakis George, *Minoan Clay Figures and Figurines*, The Archaeological Society at Athens, Library No 219, Athens 2001

Rethemiotakis Giorgos and Englezou Maria, *Το Γεωμετρικό Νεκροταφείο της Έλτυνας*, Ηράκλειο 2010

Sakellarakis Yannis and Sapouna-Sakellaraki Efi, *Archanes. Minoan Crete in a New Light*, 2 vols, Athens 1997

Sakellarakis Yannis and Sapouna-Sakellaraki Efi, *Το Ιδαίο Άντρο. Ιερό και Μαντείο*, Αθήνα 2013

Shaw Josef W., *Elite Minoan Architecture. Its Development at Knossos, Phaistos and Malia*, Philadelphia 2015

Warren Peter and Hankey Vronwey, *Aegean Bronze Age Chronology*, Bristol 1989

Watrous Livingston Vance, *Minoan Crete: An Introduction*, Cambridge 2021

FIGURE CREDITS

Exhibits photos: © Ministry of Culture-Archaeological Museum of Heraklion • Photos of archaeological sites: © Ministry of Culture / Organization for the Management and Development of Archaeological Funds (ODAP), Ephorate of Antiquities of Heraklion • Fig. 107: Photography archive of Aik. Athanasaki • Fig. 139: Photography archive of Chrysostomos Stefanakis. • Fig. 290, 298: Archaeological Museum of Heraklion, courtesy of excavator Kal. Galanakis • Fig. 297, 302: Archaeological Museum of Heraklion, courtery of excavator Ev. Grammatikakis • Images of introductory pages 1-17: Photography archive of the Archaeological Museum of Heraklion, archive of A. Evans/Oxford (p. 8 up, 10, 12) and private collections • Page 8, down: D. Baud-Bovy, Fr. Boissonnnas, De Cyclades en Crète au gré du vent, Geneva, Boissonnas X Co,1919 (Library of the Aik. Laskaridi Foundation, Με το βλέμμα των Περιηγητών, Travelogues.gr) • Page 17: «Crete-Egypt», Ministry of Culture-Archaeological Museum of Heraklion, Athens 2000 (Archive of A. Di Vita) • Fig. 100: design by R. Koehl, Aegean Bronze Age Rhyta (design by R. Porter), INSTAP, 2006 • Fig. 124: design and fig. 84: Corpus der Minoischen und Mykenischen Siegel, II,7 • Designs Fig. 98, 143: Thomas Fanourakis • Design Fig. 75 left: K. Astrinaki • Photographers: Giannis Patrikianos, Giannis Papadakis-Ploumidis, Chrysostomos Stefanakis, Deukalion Manidakis, Thanos Kartsoglou, Giannis Velegrakis, Moses Kapon.

CREATIVE DIRECTOR: **MOSES KAPON**
ARTISTIC DESIGNER: **RACHEL MISDRAHI-KAPON**
EDITING BY: **MARIOANNA LOUKA**
DTP: **ELENI VALMA, MINA MANTA, EVGENIA STASSINAKI**
PROCESSING OF ILLUSTRATIONS: **MICHALIS TZANNETAKIS**
PRINTING-BINDING: **PRINTER TRENTO** (Trento), ITALIA